A SHORT HISTORY OF INDIA

A SHORT HISTORY OF INDIA

BY

MAHAMAHOPADHYAYA

HARA PRASAD SASTRI, M.A.

GYAN

Published by

Gyan Publishing House
5, Ansari Road
Daryaganj, New Delhi-110002
Phone: 011-47034999, 9811692060
E-mail: books@gyanbooks.com

Distribution Network
gyanbooks.com
India, USA, Canada, UK, Australia

ISBN: 978-93-6280-930-8 (HB)
First Published, 1907

2nd Impression 2024

Printed at: Gyan Press, Delhi.

A SHORT HISTORY OF INDIA
Author: HARA PRASAD SASTRI

A SHORT HISTORY OF INDIA

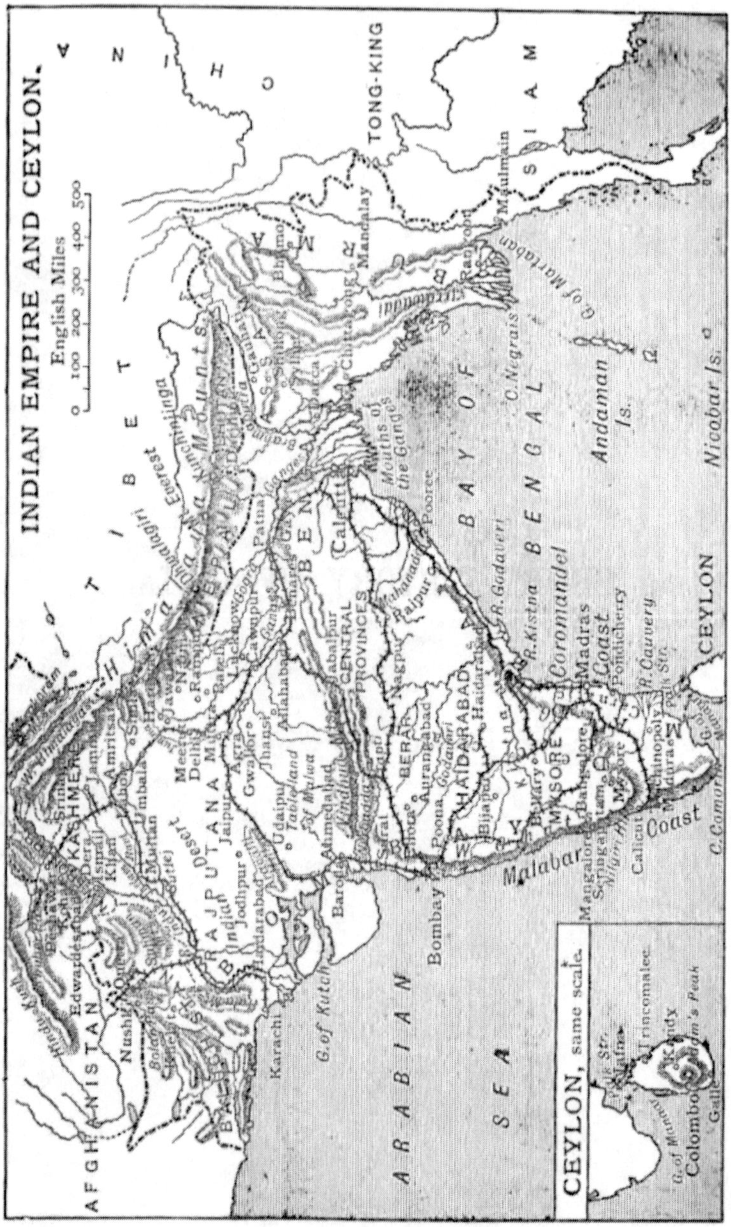
INDIAN EMPIRE AND CEYLON.
English Miles
0 100 200 300 400 500
TIBET
CHINA
TONG-KING
SIAM
AFGHANISTAN
KASHMIR
RAJPUTANA
CENTRAL PROVINCES
HAIDARABAD
MYSORE
BERAR
BAY OF BENGAL
ARABIAN SEA
Bombay
Calcutta
Madras
Karachi
Delhi
Agra
Poona
Nagpur
Mandalay
Rangoon
Maulmain
Andaman Is.
Nicobar Is.
Malabar Coast
Coromandel Coast
Pondicherry
G. of Kutch
G. of Martaban
Mouths of the Ganges
CEYLON
CEYLON, same scale.
Trincomalee
Colombo
Galle

A SHORT HISTORY OF INDIA

BY

MAHĀMAHOPĀDHYĀYA

HARA PRASĀD ŚĀSTRI, M.A.

Principal, Sanskrit College; Philological Secretary, Asiatic Society of Bengal; Fellow of the Calcutta University; Member of the R.A. Society of Great Britain and Ireland

LONDON

BLACKIE & SON, LIMITED, 50 OLD BAILEY, E.C.

GLASGOW DUBLIN BOMBAY

1907

PUBLISHERS' NOTE

In this book Professor Shastri presents the reader with a vivid and intelligibly coherent account of the vastly complicated racial, religious, social, and political movements that have produced the India of to-day. The presentation of the historical facts here given has the recommendation of being perfectly free from prejudice, or even bias.

CONTENTS

BOOK I.—EARLY HISTORY

BOOK II.—STRUGGLES FOR DOMINION

BOOK III.—THE EUROPEANS IN INDIA

BOOK IV.—BRITISH EMPIRE IN INDIA

A SHORT HISTORY OF INDIA

BOOK I.—EARLY HISTORY

CHAPTER I

INTRODUCTORY

History of India.—The history of India is the history of the various races inhabiting it, the story of the steps by which they came to have their present position among Indian peoples assigned to them, and by which the dominion of the whole of India has been secured by the British nation. At some period or other of its history, the Hindus, the Buddhists, the Scythians, the Dravidians, the Guptas, the Pathans, and the Mughals attempted to establish for themselves a universal empire, but their success was at best temporary and partial. The history of India means the history of successive partial attempts at unification followed by a speedy dismemberment, and by the rise of small kingdoms all over the land: such is the history of the rise and fall of the Gupta empire, and the history of the rise and fall of the Pathan empire was similar, as was also that of the Mughal empire.

British Empire in India.—No Indian empire until the British lasted in vigour for more than a hundred years, and none comprehended the whole of India. The British Indian empire, on the other hand, has already lasted more than a hundred years, and has not only comprehended the whole of the continent of India, but has gone beyond it in every direction. In the east, it includes the greater portion of the Indo-Chinese Peninsula; in the west, it includes Beluchistan,

Chitral, and other places; in the north, Ladak; and in the south, various islands of the Indian Ocean. It is still in its pristine vigour. It goes on centralizing departments of administration, imparting education, teaching improvements in agriculture, commerce, and manufacture, and regulating various departments of human life in a manner never contemplated by the rulers of any previous Indian empire. It is powerful abroad as well as at home. It completely protects the country from foreign invasion, and maintains perfect order within its borders, restraining the violent and punishing the law-breaker. India never enjoyed so long a period of peace and repose, and never devoted herself to civic improvements with greater zeal than during the last century.

Failure of Previous Empires.—The object of the historian of India is to find out the causes of the failures of so many previous attempts made by so many different races to establish a settled dominion, and the causes of the success of the British. The early history of India is the history of mighty individuals, who partly by their character and genius, and partly by taking advantage of some social, political, or religious revolution of their time, rose above their contemporaries and founded empires. These empires lasted usually only as long as their founders lived. As soon as they breathed their last, their ambitious subordinates broke down all bonds of authority. If their sons or grandsons were men of ability, they might avert the speedy fall of the empire; but an end was sure to come, as a succession of able rulers in the same family is a rare occurrence. Never did the races inhabiting India learn to subordinate all consideration of self to the public weal. There was something of clan spirit, something of tribal unity, but no national feeling.

Differences of British Empire.—The case is quite the reverse with the British Empire. Each Briton considers himself part and parcel of one vast body politic, the weal and woe of which is far more important than that of his own individual self; and accordingly he merges his individual feelings in the feeling of nationality. In literature and science Indians have done much. They have succeeded especially in those departments of art and science in which an individual can with success apply his genius. But whenever organization was necessary, and wherever individual effort was not enough, the Indians have failed.

Differences between British and Indians.—Scientific experiments often require organized effort, organized means, and organized energy, and in such cases the Indian seems helpless. So far as observation goes, he is very keen and of quick comprehension. His experiments are few, and he has no idea of men working for centuries on one idea. The British, on the other hand, never consider any expenditure of men, money, and exertion useless which leads to the discovery of truth by experiment. Herein lies the intellectual superiority of the Britons to the Indians. In morals and religion a Briton is more self-reliant, more sympathetic, more tolerant than an Indian. This political, intellectual, and moral superiority of Britons is the secret of their success in India.

Reasons for British Success.—I propose in these few pages to show wherein the Indians are wanting and where Britons are not wanting; wherein Indians have failed and Britons succeeded. I will dwell upon the strong and weak points of all the principal races inhabiting India, as well as the strong and weak points of their present rulers. A study of the past history of these two widely different races will convince a right-thinking man that though India and Britain were equally inhabited by a variety of races, the Indian races have striven to keep their individuality and to keep up their hatred for their neighbours, while the races in Britain merged their individuality and fused themselves into one nationality. At the time of need an Indian finds very few friends, while his opponents in his own country are many; but in his time of need a Briton finds all Britons his friends; and he has almost no opposition to meet with at home.

CHAPTER II

THE RACES INHABITING INDIA

India is inhabited by various races, who entered the country at different periods of time and from different directions. The black Dravidians, inhabiting the Deccan and Southern India, came from the east at some early period long before the beginning of history. The Mongolians, inhabiting the north-eastern corners of India, came from Mongolia and China through Tibet and the south-eastern provinces of the Chinese empire.

Aryans.—The Aryans, who form the vast majority of the influential classes, entered India from the west, at a time estimated at from 4000 B.C. to 1500 B.C. The Shemitic races came in the train of Muhammadan conquest from the west. From beyond the north-western corner of India, at various periods of Indian history, there came men of various races. None of these was very numerous. Those who came first have merged into the Aryan population, but those who came later can still be traced as distinct. And, last of all, within the last four hundred years, came the Aryan races from Europe by sea. In the beginning, commerce was their great object; but they all strove for supremacy by sea and by land. None, however, achieved so marked a success as the British.

Dravidians.—Of the history of the Dravidian races we know almost nothing. Scholars think that they were the earliest settlers in India. The vast majority have adopted Aryan civilization, and the rest are still to be found everywhere in hills and jungles in Central and Southern India. But they seem to have had their last kingdoms in the extreme south of India, in the Pandya and Kerala countries, where property descends not to the son but to the daughter.

Mongolians.—Of the emigration of Mongolian races into India in ancient times we know nothing. But we find the whole of the eastern ranges of the Himalayas and the hills to the east of Bengal inhabited by this square-faced, flat-nosed race. They seem to have come during the tenth, eleventh, and twelfth centuries, when the Mongolians were the masters of Tibet, and the Tibetans a vigorous and conquering race, after their Buddhism was reformed by the great Indian monk, Dipankara.

Hindus.—It would not be possible to speak thus summarily of the Aryan or Shemitic immigrations into India. Their immigrations form the great periods of Indian history. The Aryan period, generally called the Hindu period, commenced some thousand years before Christ, and lasted till the eighth century, when the Muhammadans began to come. The period from the eighth century to the eighteenth, generally called the Muhammadan period, is a period of struggle between Hindus and Muhammadans for supremacy in India, with varied success, ending in the subversion of both by the English.

Europeans.—The Portuguese, the Dutch, the French, and the British came from Europe in very recent times. They all tried to found an empire, but only the British succeeded.

CHAPTER III

THE ARYANS

Aryan Migration.—The Aryans are said to be the youngest of the races in the world. Their original home is supposed to have been somewhere to the east of the Caspian. Such, at least, was the opinion held by scientists till recently. Thence they sent forth colonies to the west, and peopled the whole of Europe. Those that remained behind, the possessors of all the Aryan wealth of speech, religion, and ideas, early divided themselves into two parties, the Perso-Aryans and the Indo-Aryans. One migrated to Persia, and the other to India. The date of these migrations is variously estimated. Some say they took place about 4000 years before Christ; others about 1500 before Christ. Truth seems to lie between the two.

The Rig Veda.—The Indo-Aryans came to the Punjab. It was in the Punjab that they sang their earliest known hymns, the hymns of the Rig Veda. In these hymns they speak of an ancient home; they speak of the Indus, Chenab, Jehlam, Ravi, and Sutlej. They pray to their gods for brave progeny, and large breeds of cattle, sheep, and other animals. They speak of their wars with a black-skinned, flat-nosed enemy. They speak of offering libations of the juice of the Soma-plant, an exhilarating drink, but not inebriating. In these hymns we find seven great families of Rishis taking an important part in the affairs of life; and the Brahmans of the present day still believe that they are lineally descended from these seven Rishis.

Castes and Conquests.—The Aryans having conquered the original black inhabitants of the Punjab, seem to have developed a social organization with four castes, namely, the Brahmans (men with intellectual culture), Kshatriyas (warriors), Vaisyas (traders and agriculturists)—all these being Aryans—and the Sudras, the dark people who submitted to them. They seem to have made a halt on the river Saraswati—a river which has now been lost in the sands of the Indian desert. From the Saraswati they seem to have advanced in a semicircle, first to Rohilkhand, Delhi, Mathura, and Jaipur, then to Oudh, Allahabad, Bundelkhand, and parts of Gujerat and Malwa. Their third stage of emigration comprehended the whole of Northern India, and at the fourth stage we find them crossing over the Vindhya mountains and settling first in the Berars, and then spreading gradually over the entire peninsula. The further they went from their original home in the Punjab, the larger was the number of their non-Aryan subjects. In later works we find the mention of a fifth caste, the Antyajas, who are considered below Sudras, and whose service was not acceptable to the three Aryan castes.

Civilization.—In spreading over the vast continent the Hindus developed arts, manufacture, commerce, and last of all they developed a literature in the widest sense of the term, comprehending the rudiments of grammar, prosody, pronunciation, music, law, ritual, astronomy, philology, and even geometry. They composed various Vedic works, in which they embodied not only the rules for their sacrifices, both simple and elaborate, but also their speculation on the great problems of life, even their metaphysical ideas of the Creator, of the soul, &c.

Kingship.—At the time of the Vedas, the head of the family was both its priest and its ruler. At a subsequent stage, the priestly office was monopolized by Brahmans. So the head of the family was left as its sole ruler. Gradually, however, these family headships changed into clan headships, and clan headships into kingships. Indian kings were enjoined by their Sastras, or legal treatises, never to remain contented with their own possessions, but always to strive for increase of territory. Thus, from a very early time, there was a perpetual strife amongst the Aryan kings. The Kshatriya race is said to have disappeared in consequence of the constant strife amongst themselves.

CHAPTER IV

HINDU LITERATURE

Hindu Literature.—The Puranas or legendary history of the Hindus, the story-books, the great epics, and even the later Vedic works, are full of stories of the strife of kings and other rulers. They went to war with each other on the slightest grounds, often merely because they were strong and their enemies were weak. Disquiet and unrest were the order of the day. The epics celebrate the deeds of two great Kshatriya families, one at Ayodhya (Ajodhya), on the Gogra, and the other at Hastina, in the province of Delhi.

The Ramayana.—The Ramayana celebrates the glories of Rama, a king of Ajodhya and an incarnation of Vishnu, who, to save his father from the indignity of breaking a promise, went into voluntary exile with his wife in the wilds of Southern India. There he met with many adventures and endured many sufferings, the worst of them being the abduction of his wife Sita by the king of Ceylon, the head of the man-eating ogres. Rama allied himself with the monkeys, a black and shaggy race inhabiting Southern India, and with their help threw a stone bridge over the sea, and crossed over to Ceylon. There he killed the king and a large number of his sons and grandsons, placed a friend of his own on the throne, and rescued his wife. Then he returned home, where his affectionate brother welcomed him with open arms, and he ruled his kingdom well for a long time. Rama was represented as the ideal man and ideal ruler. He was entirely good; but even he was not free from that spirit of active hostility to those of a different race, which from the earliest times has been the plague of India. He is said to have organized an aggressive expedition against the Gandharvas in the west of the Punjab, simply because they were a prosperous and wealthy nation.

The Mahabharata.—The other epic, the Mahabharata, is partly taken up with the story of a civil war between the claimants of the throne of Hastina. The original king of Hastina had two sons. The elder was born blind; so his claim was set aside, and his younger brother was placed on the throne. Both the brothers were married, and had many children; but the younger died early, and for a time the kingdom was governed by a regent. Having attained their majority, the children of both brothers claimed the throne, and being unable to settle matters peacefully, a destructive war arose. They had friends all over the then Aryanized India, and their friends joined them. Several hundred thousands of men were killed. The sons of the younger brother succeeded to the throne. Only one great family held aloof, the Jadus of Dwarka; but they, too, quarrelled amongst themselves, and were very nearly annihilated. The Puranas piteously say that from their time the Kshatriyas never recovered their former power, but that they dragged on a sort of existence till they were extirpated in historic times by the Nandas of Pataliputra.

CHAPTER V

BUDDHA

Birth and Names.—When the Kshatriyas were thus powerless, there was born in a remote corner of Central India a great man, who revolutionized the destinies not only of India but of the whole of Asia, and whose followers even at the present moment outnumber the professors of any other religion. This great man was Buddha. He is often called Gautama, because he belonged to the clan Gautama. He is called Sakya, because he was of the family of the Sakyas. He is called a Buddha, because he was enlightened. He was by birth of the Kshatriya or warrior caste. At the foot of the Himalayas there was in those days a city, which from a distance looked like a piece of white cloud among the hills. This was the capital of Buddha's father, who governed a small principality and claimed descent from the Ikshakus of Ajodhya.

Buddha

Childhood and Training.—Buddha from his early childhood showed signs of genius, but, alas! he also showed signs of a contemplative turn of mind. He preferred sitting in the shadow of the woods, lost in thought, to playing games like other boys of his age. There were not wanting old people to warn the king that his child might take to a mendicant life. The king, therefore, nurtured his son in luxury; gave him palaces, gardens, dresses, perfumes, horses, dolls; married him to a handsome girl, and never allowed him to know of the miseries of human existence.

Sorrows of Existence.—One day when the prince was

passing from the palace to a garden, he found a decrepit old man on the road. He asked his charioteer who this man was. The charioteer explained that every man is subject to old age, with all its accompanying infirmities. The prince fell into a sad reverie and returned to his palace. On a second occasion he saw on the road a sick man prostrated with fever, and having learned from his coachman that all are liable to sickness, he returned very melancholy. On the third occasion he saw a corpse, and his sorrow knew no bounds. On a fourth occasion he found a cheerful man with a shaven head and a yellow robe. On enquiring who this man was, the prince was told that he was a mendicant, that he had renounced all pleasure, all selfish desires, and led a life of self-denial, and was very cheerful. The prince thereupon thought that he too should like to be a mendicant.

Renunciation.—At this time a child was born to him, and finding that the ties of the world were becoming stronger, he resolved to break them altogether. Once he rose at midnight, resolved to renounce the world; but his eyes fell on the face of the child sleeping in its mother's bosom. The sight moved him. He was on the point of giving way, when his resolution returned, and with steady steps he left his bedroom; he left the palace; he went to the stables; took out his favourite horse; and rode fast in a direction south and east. When the day dawned, he found that his dress might lead to his being recognized; so he exchanged it for that of a peasant, cut off his beautiful hair, and rode forth as a mendicant. He went from teacher to teacher seeking to learn from them the way of salvation.

Wanderings.—He wandered for six years, and had many disciples; but he was not satisfied. In the beginning of the seventh year he sat down under a great bo-tree at Bodh Gaya, and there remained in a meditative posture for nearly six years. He gradually reduced the quantity of food he took, and then gave it up altogether. His disciples left him, thinking that he was dead; but finding at last that all these hard practices were of no avail, he rose from his seat, went to the river, gave himself a dip in it, and ate. Eating gradually caused his health to return, and he speculated on. One day the great truth flashed upon him that it is useless to practise austerities, and that it is equally useless to seek happiness in the enjoyment of all the luxuries of the world. Truth lies between.

Teachings.—Possessed of this grand idea, he went forth to preach. He found his old pupils at Benares. He converted them. He preached for forty years, and converted many thousands of men and women. There were mendicants before him; there were renunciations of the world before him; but he was the first to organize a monastic order. He roamed in Magadha (Behar) and elsewhere, and converted the kings of the various countries to his faith. He converted his wife, his stepmother, and his son. At the age of eighty he was proceeding towards Kapilavastu, but at Kusinagara (Kasia) he was attacked with dysentery, and there, lying at full length with his face turned to the right, he died between two sal-trees. His last words were addressed to Ananda, his nephew and constant attendant.

CHAPTER VI

ASOKA AND HIS SUCCESSORS

Buddhist Sects.—Some years after the death of Buddha, his followers were divided into eighteen different sects. These flourished in different parts of India, and had slightly varying doctrines, both as to the main ideas on which Buddhism is based, and as to the outward observances to be prescribed to the disciples. Soon after his death the kingdoms of India grew into large monarchies, and at last the monarchies developed into an empire. The empire was ruled, not by the Kshatriyas as of old, but by Sudras. The Brahmans pursued their intellectual and religious speculations as before, and various other forms of faith grew up along with Brahmanism and Buddhism.

Asoka's Descent.—The most important of the Buddhist sects was the Therabadis, that is, the sect which believed in the doctrines of elder monks. This sect was favoured by the greatest Buddhist monarch, Asoka. Asoka was the grandson of Chandra Gupta, the founder of the Maurya dynasty. After the departure of Alexander the Great, Chandra took possession of the Punjab, and gradually made himself master of the Magadha empire. He was himself a Sudra, but he was devotedly attached to a Brahman statesman, Chanakya.

His Aims.—Chanakya for a time served Chandra Gupta as his minister, and helped him in acquiring, regulating, and consolidating an empire extending from the Indus to the Brahmaputra. Asoka inherited this empire, but his ambition was great, so he invaded and conquered Kalinga. He spent the first nine years of his reign in a warfare, in which nearly a million human beings were killed; and the whole of Eastern India was reduced to great misery. The sight of this misery touched the heart of Asoka; and though he does not seem, on account of his sympathy with the people's sufferings, to have given up the idea of conquering, yet he became a pious man. He tried sincerely to make his subjects prosperous and happy, and to infuse into them modern religious culture.

Adopts Buddhism.—The early faith of Asoka cannot be ascertained. At first he appears to have been a seeker for truth, and he seems to have tolerated and encouraged the doctors of various of the religions existing in his empire. But at last he became a Buddhist and a Therabadi. His preceptor, Upa Gupta, known in Pali as Tisya Magyaliputtya, convened a grand meeting of the Therabadis and presided at it. This meeting settled the doctrines of the sect, and gave an impetus to it which has lasted up to the present day.

Asoka sent missionaries into the Himalayan regions, the Indo-Chinese Peninsula, and Southern India. Some of his missionaries were Greeks from Bactria, but all were inspired with a laudable zeal for doing good to mankind. Not satisfied with sending missionaries of different races, Asoka made his own sons and daughters assume the yellow robe of the Buddhist monks, and sent them forth as missionaries. His son, Mahendra, went to preach in Ceylon, where he is still regarded as the great apostle of the Buddhist faith. His daughter carried a twig of the great bo-tree under which Buddha obtained enlightenment, to Ceylon, and planted it there. The tree is still in existence: it is now a giant which covers nearly a square mile of land, and its branches are supported not only by tendrils, but also by pillars of stone, iron, brass, and other metals, placed there by the zeal of devotees.

Becomes a Missionary.—Not satisfied even with these efforts to spread the faith, Asoka himself assumed the yellow robe, and sent missives to princes and governors in distant parts of his empire, urging them to exert themselves in the interest of Buddhism. In one of his inscriptions addressed to the monks of Magadha, he expresses his anxiety for the permanence of the good religion. His inscriptions are to be found all over India, from the Khyber Pass to the Northern Circars, from the Himalayas to the Mysore country. They breathe a spirit of tolerance, and a zeal for the improvement of the moral tone of his subjects, which is rare in the world's history. His sympathies were not confined to the human race, but extended to the whole animal creation.

His Reforms.—He established hospitals for men and animals in his own dominions, and exhorted his friends, the Greek kings of Syria, Egypt, and Macedonia, and the Dravidian kings of Pandya, Chola, and Chera, countries in Southern India, to set up similar hospitals in their territories. To ensure the permanency of the Buddhist faith, he is said to have erected eighty-four thousand stupas in various parts of India, containing relics of Buddha and his great followers. Many of these are still to be found in Nepal and in Northern India. The Nepalese say that they have still preserved one monastery built by Asoka, and another by his daughter, Charumati.

His Empire and Successors.—Asoka's empire was vast; but it did not comprehend the whole of India, for the kings of Southern India are spoken of as his friends. He reigned for thirty-seven years, but within forty years of his death the empire was broken up, and the last king of his line entrusted his government entirely to his commander-in-chief, Pushpamitra. The latter supported the falling empire for a time, and fought bravely against the Bactrian Greeks, who not only took possession of the Punjab, but advanced under Menander as far as Mathura (Muttra) on the Jumna.

End of Dynasty.—Pushpamitra returned to the capital after a brilliant campaign, and the king thought it fit to give him a grand reception. At the reception there was a review of the entire army of the Maurya empire; and, when the attention of the spectators was directed to the doings of the soldiers, one of them shot an arrow at the king, who was killed on the spot. Pushpamitra was a party to the plot to kill the king, and he at once took possession of the empire, installed his son, Agnimitra, on the throne, and removed the capital to Malwa. Thus, by the treachery of one of its generals, was brought to an end the dynasty of Chandra Gupta and of Asoka his grandson.

CHAPTER VII

THE ANDHRAS AND THE GREEKS

Anarchy.—Pushpamitra's kingdom did not fare any better than its predecessor. Vasudeva, the Brahman minister of one of Pushpamitra's successors, finding the king devotedly attached to his chief queen, sent a woman to him, dressed in her robes, and she assassinated the king in his own palace.

The Andhras.—Since the death of Asoka a new enemy, the Dravidian Andhras, were gathering strength in the Deccan. They had made themselves masters of the table-land. Finding the monarchy of Northern India torn by dissensions, they now issued from Dhanakataka, in the south-eastern corner of what are now the Nizam's Dominions, and swept everything before them. Asoka's, Vasudeva's, and Pushpamitra's families were all involved in the ruin. In the first century before, and the first century after, the Christian era, the Andhras were the most powerful kings in the country. But they had soon to face a terrible enemy in the Scythians, who at that time invaded India and settled in the Punjab.

Alexander's Invasion.—From the very earliest times the Punjab seems to have been the first part of India to suffer from foreign invasion. The Persians invaded it in the sixth century and included it in their vast empire. Then came the Greeks under Alexander the Great, who had tough fighting with the Kshatriya rulers, who had succeeded in expelling the Persians. One of them, Porus, offered a stern resistance to the Macedonian conqueror; but was at last overcome, and brought as a prisoner into Alexander's presence. Alexander asked him how he wanted to be treated. Porus proudly replied, as a king. Alexander was so greatly pleased with this dignified reply, that he not only restored his possessions to him, but enlarged them by the addition of other conquered territories.

Alexander the Great

The Greeks.—Alexander remained in the Punjab for two years, and then returned to the west viâ Beluchistan. He left his fleet in the Indus under his admiral. This admiral made a voyage through the Arabian Sea and the Persian Gulf, and discovered many new countries for the Greeks. Immediately after the departure of Alexander, Chandra Gupta took possession of the Punjab, and it remained in his family for about a hundred years. Then the Greeks, under their king Eukratides, again came, not from the distant Macedonia, but from the nearer Bactria, and made themselves masters of the Punjab. The Scythians, who had driven the

Greeks from Bactria, and compelled them to seek shelter in the Punjab, continued to follow them; and, before they had

Silver Coin of Eukratides

settled, pressed into the Punjab and founded one of the largest empires in Asia.

Andhras and Scythians.—The Andhras came into conflict with the Scythians, not on the borders of the Punjab, not in Central India, but in Malwa, Guzerat, and in the Mahratta country. India was divided into two hostile camps, the east and south against the west and north. The conflict lasted long, and in the end both were exhausted and ruined.

Kanishka.—The greatest monarch of the Scythians was Kanishka. His capital was at Purushapur or Peshawar. His empire extended from beyond the Narbada to far-off Tartary. It is not known what the religion of the Scythians was. They were most likely the Zoroastrians of the later time, with Magi for their priests. Kanishka, however, became a Buddhist, and convened a great meeting of the Buddhists at Jalandar. He is said to have got all the canonical books of the Buddhists written down in Sanskrit, as the books of the Kerabadis were all in Pali. Kanishka's connection helped the Buddhists, and spread their faith in China, Mongolia, Siberia, and other northern and eastern countries of Asia.

The study of Jyotisha, astronomy, received a new impetus from the Greeks and specially from the Scythians. The era, which is counted from the day of the coronation of the greatest of Scythian kings, and known in India as the *sakabda*, having been used by astronomers and astrologers, has obtained a much wider currency in India than eras founded by her own monarchs.

CHAPTER VIII

THE GUPTAS

Gupta Empire.—Out of the ruin of the Scythian and of the Andhra kingdoms rose the empire of the Guptas. The foundation of the empire dates from the year 319 of the Christian era. The capital of the empire was at Pataliputra (Patna). But latterly they had other capitals, Ajodhya in the Faizabad District and Ujjain in Gwalior. Their empire at one time included the whole of Northern and Eastern India, the Punjab, and Guzerat. There are inscriptions in Southern India in which monarchs of that country boast of their being the chief advisers of the Guptas in Southern India. They were worshippers of Vishnu and Lakshmi. Their religion was Brahmanism.

Encouragement of Learning.—They encouraged Sanskrit; the greatest poets, the greatest astronomers, the greatest philosophers of India flourished under their rule. Kalidas and Bharavi, Aryyavarta and Barahamihir, Sobaraswami and Udyotakara flourished when the Guptas were in power. Their empire lasted in great vigour till 460, and, though broken, it continued to exist till the year 606. They claimed to be Kshatriyas, but their surname shows that they belonged to the third caste, the Vaisyas. Under their dominion some of the greatest Buddhist writers flourished; but from their time onwards it was apparent that Buddhism was a losing and Brahmanism a growing faith. Commerce and manufactures flourished greatly in their time. Different industries and trades were organized, and rules were made for the conduct of the affairs of the trade and for the support of the poor members belonging to it. These trade societies or guilds also built temples and monasteries for the benefit of the various organizations.

Struggle with Hunas.—The Hunas were the great enemies of the Guptas. Under their leaders, Toraman and Mihirakula, they invaded India about the middle of the fifth century and carried ruin and devastation before them. The Gupta empire was not in a position to resist them effectively, and in a short time the Hunas occupied not only the Punjab, but the greater portion of Central India and Malwa. The Gupta empire of India really came to an end. The Guptas continued to reign, but only in the eastern portion of what had been their vast empire, though the affairs of the empire were still conducted and coins were struck in their name. Two dependent monarchies rose into prominence by their struggle against the Hunas, one at Ujjain and the other at Thaneswar.

Yasodharma.—The monarch of Ujjain, Yasodharma by name, boasts in an inscription that his dominions extend from the Himalayas to the Eastern Ghats and from sea to sea; that he was master of territories which never owned the allegiance of the Guptas, and that Mihirakula, the great Huna king, did him homage. Yasodharma is said to have defeated the Hunas with great carnage at Korcer, between Multan and Luni, in the year 534 A.D.–535 A.D.

Vikramaditya.—Some say that this Yasodharma is the great Vikramaditya of Indian tradition, who had nine learned men known as the Navaratna, or "nine gems", in his court. These nine men occupy the first position in nine different branches of knowledge. Some have doubted whether those nine distinguished men were contemporaries at all. But one thing is certain, that all of them flourished after the middle of the Gupta period, 319–606.

CHAPTER IX

HARSHABARDHAN AND BUDDHISM

Expulsion of Hunas.—The other monarch who distinguished himself by his resistance to the Hunas was Pravakarabardhan of Thaneswar. He, like Yasodharma, rebelled against the Guptas, and set up an independent monarchy on the ruins of their dominion. He expelled the Hunas from the greater part of the Punjab, but the work of expulsion was completed by his son, Rajyabardhan. The sudden rise of this family was an offence to the king of Malwa, perhaps a descendant of Yasodharma.

War between Thaneswar and Malwa.—Immediately after the death of the old king of Thaneswar, finding his eldest son engaged in a war with the Hunas, the king of Malwa invaded Kanauj, the kingdom of the son-in-law of Prabhakara, killed the king, took his wife Rajyasri a prisoner, and annexed his kingdom to Malwa. After the subjugation of the Hunas, Rajyabardhan determined to teach a lesson to the king of Malwa, and proceeded thither with an immense army. Malwa was speedily subjugated, but no trace of the conqueror's sister was found: search was made in every quarter, but in vain.

Death of Rajyabardhan.—After the conquest of Malwa, it came to the notice of the conqueror that the Gupta king of western Bengal had aided the king of Malwa. Rajyabardhan, on learning this, led his victorious army into Bengal; but the king submitted at once, on his approach, and did not hazard an engagement. He was the last of the Guptas. He showed great friendliness to Rajyabardhan, and invited him to a dinner, and there treacherously put him to death.

Harshabardhan recovers his Sister.—Rajyabardhan's army returned to Thaneswar, and Harshabardhan, his brother, vowed to wreak his vengeance on the king of Bengal. He collected as many soldiers as he could and marched towards the east. When encamped on the bank of the river Ganges, he obtained some trace of his sister. Following the track he entered the Vidhyan forests. After passing several miles through thick jungles he reached the hermitage of a Buddhist sage named Dibakara. This sage had numerous disciples, and these were engaged in studying all the various branches of knowledge. The king was greatly struck with the learning, piety, and devotion of this great monk, and asked him if he knew anything of his sister. He pointed out a disciple of his who had saved Rajyasri from self-immolation by fire. This man led the king to his sister. They met after a long time, during which they had suffered many misfortunes; and when they thought on all they had undergone, they wept bitterly.

End of Gupta Empire.—Well pleased with this sudden and almost unexpected good fortune which had followed his search, Harshabardhan proceeded to western Bengal, fought with the treacherous king, killed him, sacked his capital, and put an end to the Gupta empire in 606 A.D. Rajyasri became a disciple of Dibakara; Harshabardhan, later, followed in her steps and became a Buddhist. Buddhism again flourished for a short time.

Literature.—Harshabardhan was a great patron of learning. He patronized Vana, who wrote a history of his reign—the first historical work in Sanskrit. There are also some dramatic works attributed to this king's reign. He held regularly every fifth year an assembly of all the learned men in his empire, and used to reward them according to their merit.

Hiouen Thsang.—The great Chinese traveller, Hiouen Thsang, was present at one of these assemblies, and he gives a full description of what took place. Hiouen Thsang was a Chinese monk who, coming to India through Mongolia, Gobi, and Khotan, crossed over the Hindu Kush, and entered the country at its north-western extremity. He travelled over the entire length and breadth of India, visited all the sacred places of the Buddhists, passed through all the kingdoms forming the vast empire of Harshabardhan, remained some years at Nalanda, near Gaya, to study the sacred books with the help of the most eminent scholars of that great university, and cultivated the friendship of Harshabardhan and the eminent men forming his court.

University of Nalanda.—His description of the university of Nalanda, the most famous Buddhist monastery of India, is worth noticing. There were ten thousand students at the place; there was one building which accommodated all of them. The revenues of a hundred villages were assigned for the support of the monks, novices, and students. The old monks had rooms in the upper story, and each had one or two servants according to his need. There were lecture halls, study rooms, assembly halls, and all sorts of buildings necessary for a great place of learning like that. The whole was superintended by an elderly monk. In Hiouen Thsang's time, the superintendent was Silabhadra, aged more than eighty, who could repeat the whole of the canonical works from memory. Hiouen Thsang was delighted with what he saw. Though the greatest king of India was a Buddhist, yet Hiouen Thsang was sorry to find that Buddhism was a decaying faith.

Invasion of the Deccan.—Harshabardhan united the whole of Northern India under his rule, from Assam to Peshawar, from the Himalayas to the Vindhyas; there was none to dispute his sway. But he wanted universal monarchy, and so he invaded the Deccan, crossed the Vindhyas and the Narbada.

Overthrow of Harshabardhan.—From the fall of the Andhra empire, there had existed two great monarchies in the Deccan and Southern India. The first had its capital at Kanchi, now Conjeveram, the greatest and most beautiful of Indian cities; the other had its capital at Vatafi, in what is now the Nizam's territories. The first was the earlier and the last was the later monarchy. The kingdom of Badami was ruled by a hardy race of Rajputs, known as the Chalukyas. They were jealous of Harshabardhan's power, and were prepared to meet him. The armies met not far from the Narbada, and the Chalukyas inflicted such a terrible defeat on Harshabardhan that the northern monarch never again attempted to invade their country.

Never afterward was such a vast Hindu monarchy founded, either in Northern or in Southern India, as was the monarchy of Harshabardhan.

BOOK II.—STRUGGLES FOR DOMINION

CHAPTER I

THE STRUGGLE OF THE HINDUS AND MUHAMMADANS

Muhammadanism.—Muhammad was born in 569 A.D., and died in 632 A.D. His life was not long, but during his lifetime he created a revolution the like of which was never witnessed in this world. The hardy race of dwellers in the Arabian deserts, inspired with enthusiasm by his spirit-stirring speeches, spread his religion far into the west and into the east. The effete monarchy of Persia fell to pieces as soon as it came into hostile contact with this new enthusiasm. Within eight years of Muhammad's death, the Persian monarchy and the Zoroastrian religion were things of the past. The Muhammadans in a short time absorbed Afghanistan and Baluchistan, and were anxious to invade India.

Invasion of India.—They wanted a leader for such an adventurous expedition. That leader they found in Muhammad Bin Kasim, who on a very slight pretext led an army into Sindh, defeated in many battles the king Dahir, who offered a stubborn resistance, invested his capital, took it by storm, and sacked it. The chief cities of Sindh submitted in rapid succession, and in the course of three or four years Muhammad found himself in a position to follow up his conquest in the north and in the east. But before he could proceed further a sad fate overtook him.

Present to Khalifa.—Amongst the prisoners who fell into his hands after the fall of the capital were two daughters of the king. Muhammad sent them as a present to the Khalifa.

The elder princess was greatly enraged at the sad fate of her father, of her country, and of her religion, and she secretly vowed vengeance on the author of all her miseries. Arrived at the capital of the Khalifa, she was taken into the harem. Her great beauty attracted the attention of the Khalifa, who fell desperately in love with her; but she at once informed him that she was unworthy of his majesty, as she had already been dishonoured by his general. Roused to anger by this statement, the Khalifa at once ordered that Muhammad's dead body should be brought to him. Muhammad was assassinated, and his body, placed in a bag, was sent to the Khalifa.

Punishment of Princess.—The Khalifa took it to the beautiful princess, and she at once confessed the trick she had played to wreak her vengeance on the oppressor of her father and her country, and the Khalifa ordered that she should be beheaded. With Muhammad ended the hope of an early Muhammadan conquest of India. Sindh and Multan, however, have remained in the hands of Muhammadans ever since. Though the rulers were Muhammadans, there were certain Hindu families in these states which held many of the important offices.

CHAPTER II

RAJA BHOJ

Spread of Rajput Power.—After the fall of Harshabardhan, Northern India fell into the hands of several Rajput families, each of which became independent in one or other of the provinces. Of these Rajput families, the Paramaras of Dhara in Malwa were famous for their patronage of learning.

Raja Bhoj.—Raja Bhoj, so famous in Indian legends, ruled Malwa from 1006 to 1042. He gathered together a great library, and made large compilations in every branch of knowledge cultivated at the time in India.

The Chalukyas.—The Chalukyas of Guzerat were famous for their patronage of Jainism. The great Jain Pandit, Hema

Chandra, flourished in their court. Some of them were very tender towards animal life. Kusmara Pala closed all butchers' shops in his country, and for three years paid the butchers from the treasury sums equal to their average income.

The Palas of Magadha.—The Palas of Magadha were Buddhists. They supported two great seats of learning, namely, those of Nalanda and Vikramasila. The mission of Dipankara to Tibet has already been noticed. The rulers of all these small dynasties were builders of temples, patrons of learning, granters of lands to Brahmans and to monastic orders, and performers of various works of public utility; but they were constantly at war with one another, and they often persecuted cruelly those who professed a different religious faith.

Sura Dynasty.—The histories of the Sura and the Sena dynasties of Bengal were, however, of a very different nature. Adisur, the founder of the Sura dynasty, saw that he was ruling a country inhabited principally by Buddhists, not the pure Buddhists of Asoka's time, but professors of a religion to which the name of Buddhism could not with propriety be given. He discovered that the Brahmans of Kanauj were very learned and very pious, so he invited five of them to his court and asked them to undertake the regeneration of the country. With the Brahmans came the Kayasthas, their devoted adherents. The Brahmans and Kayasthas multiplied, and the Brahmanical faith spread rapidly all round. With their increase in number, Brahmans and Kayasthas settled in northern Bengal in the Pala dominions. These are known as Varendra Brahmans and Varendra Kayasthas.

Palas of Bengal.—The Sura dynasty lasted for many generations, and was supplanted by the Senas, who came from the south and settled at Nadia. They connected themselves with the Suras by marriage, and gradually took possession of their dominions. The Palas were at this time the chief people in northern Bengal, but they had great troubles with the Kaibartas. When at last they had very nearly subdued these troublesome rebels, the Senas came to the rescue of the

Kaibartas, and seized the whole of northern Bengal. The higher class of the Kaibartas were settled by the Senas in the southern extremity of their dominions, and thus northern Bengal was saved from their turbulence. Master of northern, western, and central Bengal, the Senas busied themselves with the conquest of Mithila and eastern Bengal.

The Sena Dynasty.—Ballal, the greatest of the Sena kings, reorganized the caste system in Bengal. He degraded some and elevated others, according to their piety towards the Brahmans. He classified the Brahmans according to their learning and piety. The highest class was known as *kulins*, the middle as *shrotriyas* (*Mukhyas* and *Gaunas*), and the lowest as Bansaj. Ballal's regulations, with slight and occasional variations, are still binding in Bengal. His son, Lakshan, was a great king. He had five great poets at his court. In early life Ballal seems to have been a Buddhist, but he was afterwards converted to Saivaism. His son was a Vaishnava, and the great Vaishnava poet, Jayadeva, received the highest honour at his court.

Spread of Brahmanism.—In Southern India the position previously held by the Chalukyas was taken for a time by the Rattas. These, again, were driven from power by a new race of Chalukyas. On the fall of these second Chalukyas, the country was divided into many kingdoms, of which those of Devagiri, Warrangal, and Dvarasamudra were the chief. A great impetus to Brahmanism came from the south. Kumarila Bhatta (about 750 A.D.) and his famous disciple, Sankaracharyya, had succeeded, by their teaching and their preaching, by the latter end of the eighth and the beginning of the ninth century, in reorganizing Vedic Hinduism, one for laymen and the other for the monastic orders. Both tried hard to bring back Brahmans to the Vedic faith, to the exclusion of Saivaism, Vaishnavism, and other religions. Neither succeeded in doing what he wanted—Saivaism, Vaishnavism, and other religions are still flourishing—but they accomplished two great things. Kumarila compelled every Brahman to conform to certain Vedic observances, and Sankar instituted a monastic order of high character, which has done much to diffuse the higher life amongst the Hindus.

Other Monastic Orders.—There are other monastic orders amongst the Hindus besides those founded by him, but they form together only a tenth of Sankara's order. Bhavabhuti, who ranks next after Kalidasa as the greatest Sanskrit poet, is said to have been a pupil of Kumarila. He was born at Padmanagar in Bundelkhand, and was an ornament of the court of the king of Kanauj. Ramanuja, the great leader of Vaishnavas in Southern India, flourished in the thirteenth century, and tried his best to found a sect rivalling that of Sankara.

CHAPTER III

AFGHAN INVASIONS

Mahmud of Ghazni.—About the end of the tenth century a small Muhammadan kingdom had been formed close to the Punjab, with its capital at Ghazni. The ruler of this little kingdom was ambitious. It took some time to consolidate the affairs of the kingdom; but, as soon as internal peace was secured, the second king of the Ghaznavide line fell on the Hindu dominion of the Punjab. The Raja of Lahore, Jaipál, was prepared for the invasion, and he offered a stubborn resistance. Later he led his troops through the passes and attacked Sabaktagin; but he was defeated, and finally compelled to pay tribute.

Conquest of Lahore and Multan.—Soon after, however, the king of Ghazni, Sabaktagin, died, and his young son, Mahmud, was engaged elsewhere, so the Raja withheld his tribute. Afterwards Mahmud came, inflicted a terrible defeat on the Raja, and compelled him to pay larger tribute. The Musalman king of Multan had been forced to pay tribute to Ghazni. He also now withheld his tribute, and Mahmud had to come and teach him a lesson. Twice defeated by the Muhammadans, the king of Lahore committed suicide. As, according to

Hindu notions, a twice-defeated king was unworthy of ruling, he solemnly made over the kingdom to his son, and ascended the funeral pyre. His son made immense preparations to resist the attack of Mahmud. All the Rajput states contributed their quota, and even ladies sent their ornaments to save their country from the invasion of foreigners. But, alas! all their efforts proved futile. In the thick of battle an arrow pierced the brain of Ananga Pal, the Raja of Lahore. On the death of their leader, the Hindus lost heart and fled. Victory remained with the Muhammadans. Mahmud raised Ananga Pal's son to the throne of Lahore, and compelled him to pay a still larger tribute. Within a few years Mahmud led several expeditions into India, and plundered Kashmir and the great temple of Nagarkot in Kangra, where he got immense booty.

Mahmud's Pillars, Ghazni

Mahmud's Treaty with Rajyapala.—Encouraged by repeated successes in the land of the five rivers, Mahmud led an expedition into Central India, and suddenly appeared before Kanauj, then ruled by a Pala king named Rajyapala. Unable to resist, the king made a virtue of necessity, and entered into a treaty with Mahmud. Mahmud left Kanauj untouched, but plundered Mathura (Muttra). The artistic buildings of Mathura attracted the attention of Mahmud, and henceforward he tried his best to adorn his capital [illegible]me the [illegible]r buildings.

Punjab Annexed.—The king of Kalanjara, annoyed at Rajyapala for making friends with a Muhammadan, invaded his territory, and killed him in battle. Mahmud returned to India to teach this insolent Raja a lesson. He plundered the country, and inflicted much misery on it; but the Raja, with the assistance of Bhoj of Dhar and other Rajput kings, gave him very great trouble. On Mahmud's way back to Ghazni the tributary Raja of Lahore offered resistance. He was deposed, and the Punjab was annexed to the Muhammadan dominions.

Expedition against Somnath.—The last of Mahmud's seventeen invasions of India was against the great shrine of Somnath, situated in the southernmost extremity of the peninsula of Kathiawar. He passed through Ajmere and Anahilpattan, the capital of Guzerat, and reached Somnath. The Raja of Guzerat opposed him, the priests of the shrine did their best to protect it, but it was in vain. Mahmud defeated the combined army, entered the temple, plundered its contents, and razed it to the ground. He returned home, and died six years after. His empire soon after fell to pieces, his family was expelled even from Ghazni, and they retired to Lahore, where they reigned for two generations, but were expelled from Lahore too by the descendant of the conqueror who had expelled them from Ghazni. Then these princes of Ghor set themselves to conquer the Punjab.

CHAPTER IV

AFGHAN INVASIONS (*Continued*)

Flight of Ghaznavites.—The conqueror who expelled the Ghaznavites from Lahore was Shahabuddin Ghori, so called because the capital of his small principality was in Ghor, a small valley not far from Ghazni. Some of his ancestors had been badly treated by the descendants of Mahmud, so the entire clan, known as the Surs, rose in rebellion against the rulers of Ghazni. Their rebellion proving successful, the Ghaznavites gave way, and the prince fled into the Punjab. Shahabuddin was the last king of this dynasty, and he was a very powerful sovereign. He easily succeeded in destroying the Ghaznavite power in the Punjab, and he entertained the design of conquering the whole of Northern India.

War with Delhi.—The Hindu kingdom bordering on his dominions was that of Delhi. It was then ruled by Prithi Roy Chauhan, the most warlike king of a most warlike race. Through his father he inherited the kingdom of Ajmere, and through his mother the kingdom of Delhi. By his own prowess he conquered nearly half the kingdom of Kalanjara. It was no easy task for Shahabuddin to fight a powerful monarch like Prithi Roy. But he had one advantage. He had great tenacity of purpose, while his rival was rather impulsive.

Defeat of Prithi Roy.—In 1189 Shahabuddin crossed the Sutlej and entered Hindustan; but he was completely defeated by the intrepid Prithi Roy at Thaneswar. He was badly wounded, too, and barely escaped with his life. He returned crest-fallen and humiliated, but he did not give up his idea. For two years he carried on his preparations, then he returned to India. His return was regarded with contempt by his rival, who thought the once-defeated Shahabuddin would be easily beaten. But his expectations were not realized. Shahabuddin proved more than a match for him. The Hindus were defeated in 1193 A.D., and Prithi Roy was slain. Delhi fell into the hands of Muhammadans, who placed Prithi Roy's son on the throne of Ajmere, but compelled him to receive a Muhammadan Resident. Next year the Muhammadans conquered Kanauj. But it took more than two years to subdue the military outposts of Kanauj in Oudh and Benares.

Conquests in Northern India.—In 1197 Muhammad's general Bakhtiyar conquered Magadha, and sacked its capital, Udantapuri. Next year he advanced into Bengal, and took Nadia. Gaur fell, and in a short time the north, west, and central parts of Bengal submitted. Thus, in the course of ten years, Shahabuddin made himself master, not only of the land of the five rivers, but of the entire Gangetic valley. This rapid conquest was a mere overrunning and military occupation. The real conquest was yet to come.

Death of Shahabuddin and Division of his Dominions.—Shahabuddin was engaged all his life in warfare, and he made many enemies among the mountain tribes of the Punjab. In the year 1206 the Ghakkars fell upon his camp on the bank of the Indus at night, and killed him. He had no heir, so his possessions in India fell to the lot of his Viceroy at Delhi, Kutabuddin. Another of his generals took possession of Sindh. Kutabuddin was the first Emperor of Delhi. He reigned for only a very short time. He had started life as a Turkish slave, and his dynasty is accordingly known as the dynasty of the slave kings. He died in 1210 A.D. His son's reign did not last long, but his son-in-law, Altamsh, reigned many years, conquered Malwa, sacked Ujjain, and destroyed the temple of Mahakal there.

Invasion by Changiz Khan.—But an unexpected enemy appeared at this time on the borders of India. This was Changiz Khan, the greatest of the rulers of the Mughal race. He united the nomad hordes of Mongolia, and in rapid succession conquered all the countries from the Baltic to the Pacific Ocean. On his approach to India, Altamsh made submission, and saved his empire from devastation.

Mughal Irruption.—Altamsh's successors were very weak. His daughter, Raziya, was the only lady that ever occupied the Muhammadan throne of Delhi (1236–1239 A.D.). The slave dynasty was for some time after this busily engaged in resisting the invasions of the Mughals. So the Hindus found this a fine opportunity of recovering much of their lost dominions. Of the successors of Altamsh, the only one deserving any notice was his son-in-law, Ghiyasuddin Balban, who afforded shelter to many of the Muhammadan princes of Turkey, Persia, and Tartary expelled from their kingdoms by the Mughals. Balban is said to have boasted that no fewer than fifteen once independent sovereigns were fed by his bounty. His cruelties and severities were remarkable.

Khilji Dynasty.—Balban's family was replaced by the Khiljis, and Alauddin was the greatest Khilji monarch of Delhi. The Mughals had by this time been converted to Muhammadanism, and many of them settled in India. The disbanded soldiers of the Muhammadan kingdoms, destroyed by the Mughals, flocked to India in quest of service. Alauddin took a very large number of these into his pay, and planned the conquest of the Deccan and of Southern India.

Conquests of Alauddin.—The first expedition he led in person, and the others were commanded by his generals. In rapid succession they subdued the monarchies of Guzerat, Malwa, Devagiri, and Dvarasamudra. He sent an army under his slave, Malik Kafur, to attack Warrangal, the capital of the Hindu kingdom of Telingana, but he could not overthrow that monarchy. His troops overran the whole of Southern India. They reached Rameswar on the east coast, and Malabar on the west coast. Alauddin was very proud of his conquest, and posed as a second Alexander. He was a very wicked monarch. He ordered the Rana of Chitor to send his beautiful wife, "Padmini", to his harem. The Rana indignantly refused; and Alauddin led an expedition to Chitor in person. He treacherously imprisoned Bhim Singh, took the capital by storm, and entered the palace only to find "Padmini", the queen, flinging herself on the funeral pile. The garrison of Chitor preferred death to submission, and the Hindu ballad tells how the queen and thirteen thousand women perished on the funeral pile.

His Death.—Alauddin had a miserable end. His favourite general is suspected of having poisoned him. Before his death he gave himself up to rage and intemperance. His family did not reign long after his death, and they were succeeded by the Tughlaks, an Indian Muhammadan family long resident in the Punjab. After Alauddin's death the actual power came into the hands of Khuzru Khan, a low-caste renegade Hindu, who murdered his patron, Malik Kafur.

CHAPTER V

PATHAN EMPIRE

House of Tughlak, 1320–1414.—The Tughlaks began well. They annexed the Mahratta kingdom of Devagiri to the Delhi empire. The founder of the dynasty, already an old man, was a wise ruler and a veteran soldier, who defended the Punjab against the invasion of the Mughals. The second king, however, of this dynasty came to the throne by killing his father, and was the very opposite of a wise ruler. He was a learned man, a poet, a critic, a philosopher, an accomplished soldier, but a very bad ruler. He was ferocious, careless of human suffering, and when opposed seemed to become mad. He collected a very large army for the conquest of China, but he had no money to defray the expenses. He issued paper money; but nobody would take it, as he had no credit. He wanted to change his capital, and twice ordered the inhabitants of Delhi to proceed to Devagiri, the capital of his choice, to which he gave the name of Daulatabad. He compelled every citizen of Delhi to leave his own house behind and to proceed to the new capital.

Quarrel with Mercenaries.—Such a ruler was not likely to brook tamely the insolence of the leaders of mercenaries of various nationalities by whose aid Alauddin had overrun India. For what he considered good reasons he ordered the massacre of seventy of these chiefs. The mercenaries rebelled. For a time Malwa, Guzerat, Sindh, and the Deccan were lost to the empire. Southern India had already gained independence under new Hindu dynasties. Under the Musalman viceroy, Bengal, too, had declared its independence, and had expelled the Musalman garrisons, and could not be subdued. Finding everything in danger, Muhammad strenuously exerted himself for several years, and pacified Malwa, Guzerat, and Sindh. His cruelties were revolting, though they were temporarily successful. He died of overwork.

Firoz Tughlak.—His successor was a good man, a good

Musalman, and a good ruler. He executed many works of public utility, converted a very large number of Hindus, specially Rajputs, to Muhammadanism, and was anxious to encourage learned men. His name was Firoz Tughlak. He left what he got from Muhammad intact, but he was forced to recognize the independence of the Muhammadan kingdoms of Bengal and the Deccan. The ruin of the empire could not be averted. On his death the governors of Guzerat, Malwa, and Sindh, and Jaunpur declared themselves independent. So Mahmud, the last king of the dynasty, ruled but a small territory round Delhi, and he was not destined to rule even this little kingdom long.

Timur's Invasion.—In 1398 a new scourge appeared in India, and destroyed even the last vestiges of the Delhi empire. Timur, with innumerable Tartar hordes, after overthrowing all the kingdoms of Central Asia, fell upon India. On his approach, Mahmud left Delhi and sought the protection of the newly-founded independent kingdom of Guzerat. Delhi was at that time torn by internal feuds, and there was no united action to check the progress of Timur. It was Timur's habit to massacre the inhabitants of any city to which he was obliged to lay siege; and, before reaching Delhi, he had already brutally put the inhabitants of six or seven Indian cities to the sword, so that as he approached the inhabitants of city after city fled precipitately with their property. The people of Delhi made a feeble attempt to oppose him, but in vain. After a slight show of resistance the citizens opened their gates on his assurance that no lives would be taken.

Sack of Delhi.—On entering Delhi, Timur proclaimed himself emperor; and immediately afterwards the sack of the place began. For five days human blood flowed in torrents, and the streets became impassable from the heaps of dead bodies left in them to rot. After a stay of fifteen days Timur left the city; and, massacring the inhabitants of Meerut on his way, proceeded to Haridvar. Here the Hindus began to harass him, and he had to cut his way, sword in hand, through the jungles at the foot of the mountains. All the way to Jamu he was greatly harassed by the Hindus of this wild region. From Jamu he returned by the same road by which he had come. Famine, anarchy, and plague marked his route. Of all the enemies of humanity Timur and Changiz were the greatest. They were equally cruel; but Timur was, in addition, treacherous.

End of Dynasty.—After Timur had left India, Delhi remained desolate for two months. Then Ekbal, the minister of Mahmud, took possession of it. Internal feuds broke out afresh, and Ekbal was the first victim. Mahmud returned to his capital, and reigned there nominally up to 1412. He had already ceased to coin money as emperor of Delhi; never sat on the throne, and relinquished the imperial authority altogether.

Break-up of Empire.—Thus the political power of the early Musalmans, which under Shahabuddin had spread over the whole of Northern India, and under Alauddin over nearly all Southern India, rose almost to the position of universal empire in India, but did not continue in that condition for more than fifty years. The genius of Alauddin made it an empire, but his successors could not retain the power. The empire broke up, and there was a score of petty independent kingdoms, Hindu as well as Muhammadan.

CHAPTER VI

HINDU AND MUHAMMADAN KINGDOMS

The Kingdom of Vijayanagar, 1118–1565.—The first to throw off the Muhammadan yoke was Vir Bukka, the founder of Vijayanagar. The capital of Vijayanagar was Hampa (Byayanagar), a city situated by the holy lake of Pampa, so famous in the Ramayana. The ruined city is in the Bellary district of Madras presidency. Besides its political achievements this kingdom is famous for bringing about a Vedic revival. Sayana and Madhava, two brothers, the spiritual guides of Bukka, commented upon the four Vedas and wrote many works. The effect of this Vedic revival was wide-spread. It made the Brahmans south of Krishna thoroughly conversant with the Vedas, and trained them in the manner of the old Vedic Rishis. The wave of the revival reached even Hindustan and Bengal.

The Struggle with the Muhammadans.—The capital of the kingdom, situated behind a range of hills, is described as one of the most magnificent in the world. The ruins cover nine square miles, if Kumalpur on the south, and Anagundi, the seat of the dynasty, be included. They are exceedingly picturesque to look at. The rulers of Vijayanagar were the last and most powerful enemies of the Muhammadans. They it was that offered the fiercest resistance to the spread of the Muhammadan conquest. In northern Madras, between the mouth of the Krishna and the Tungabhadra, were fought for nearly two hundred years the most furious and bloody battles between the Hindus and the Muhammadans. But the kingdom of Vijayanagar had at last to succumb to the combined effort of several Muhammadan kingdoms.

Kings of Warangal.—Alauddin did not subvert the dynasty of Hindu kings reigning at Warangal. That kingdom, situated to the east of the Hydrabad territories, included the Northern Circars. It also continued to struggle hard against the Muhammadans, but had to submit at last. The kings of Warangal patronized Sanskrit learning. Mallinath, the famous commentator, flourished at their court. One of the kings had left behind him a huge compilation of Hindu rituals known as Prataparudri.

Bahmani Kingdom.—The Bahmani kingdom was founded by a Musalman who was servant to a Brahman at Delhi. In honour of his master the Muhammadan assumed the title of Bahmani; and it is said that, as a dynasty, they never killed Brahmans, though they were great persecutors of the Hindus. There were a few kings of this dynasty who were above the average, but there was one of their ministers, Mahmud Gawan, whose biography should be studied with care.

Mahmud Gawan.—Few characters so unselfish, so modest, so learned, and so able are to be found in Indian history. He came to India as a merchant, and, by sheer force of ability and by integrity, became the foremost man in the Bahmani State. He spent all his wealth in public charities, in founding schools and colleges, in building mosques and hospitals, and in helping the learned and the distressed. He subjugated Telingana and made it a province of the Bahmani kingdom. Up to this time the whole sea-coast from Bengal to Guzerat had been in the hands of the Hindus. But Mahmud Gawan, by annexing the Konkan and the Northern Circars, extended the Muhammadan power from sea to sea, and thus separated the Hindu kingdoms from one another. The fiscal arrangements of Mahmud Gawan, some of which are still in force, were excellent, and so was his organization of the educational, judicial, and military departments. But all his noble qualities and disinterested services to the State could not save him from the malignity of the Deccani party.

Muhammadans capture Kanchi.—It was about this time that the Musalmans invaded the holy city of Kanchi or Conjeveram, which had hitherto remained in the undisturbed possession of the Hindus. Sultan Muhammad Shah, the thirteenth Bahmani king, was present at the capture of this beautiful Hindu city, and he killed the high-priest, a venerable Brahman, with his own hand. People thought the Bahmani dynasty came to an end as a punishment for this killing of a Brahman.

Kingdom of Guzerat.—Of the small kingdoms of Northern India, Guzerat was the most considerable. It was ruled throughout its existence by one dynasty of converted Rajputs noted for their zeal for the Muhammadan faith. They destroyed the temple of Somnath; and they adorned their capital, Ahmadabad, with palaces and mosques that are still admired by visitors. They often claimed supremacy over the neighbouring rulers of Khandes, Ahmadnagar, and Malwa, and they were constantly at war with the Ranas of Chitor, who were anxious to expel the Muhammadans from the Madhyades, Central India, the Aryan country or sacred land of the Hindus.

Bahadur Shah.—Bahadur Shah, the most popular of Guzerati kings, sacked Chitor about 1530, and the Rana sought the protection of Humayun, Emperor of Delhi, who defeated Bahadur in the battle of Mandu, and compelled him to take refuge with the Portuguese. Humayun conquered the whole of Guzerat; but he was soon dispossessed of his empire by Sher Khan Afghan, and Bahadur then regained his kingdom and his independence.

Dynasties in Malwa.—Two dynasties ruled in Malwa, one after another. They were constantly engaged in attempts to wrest the hill forts from the Rajputs. The Rajputs attained great influence in this kingdom, and were often at the head of its affairs. Medini Ray of Chanderi was specially an object of jealousy to the Muhammadan nobles. The rulers of Malwa were often at war with the Ranas of Mewar, and Bahadur Shah of Guzerat conquered and annexed Malwa in 1531. From this time the history of Malwa is full of confusion.

Kingdom of Jaunpur.—The kingdom of Jaunpur extended from Bengal to Kanauj. It was founded by a Khauja, who received from Mahmud Tughlak the title of Malik-us-Sharq, or "the Governor of the East". The dynasty, founded by the adopted son of the Khauja, is known as the Sharqui dynasty. They are celebrated in India on account of the beautiful architecture with which they adorned their cities and courts.

The Ranas of Chitor.—The story of the destruction of Chitor by Alauddin has already been told. In the course of a few years Hambira succeeded in expelling the Muhammadans. The dynasty founded by him was a very ambitious one. Rulers of this dynasty even meditated the expulsion of the Muhammadans from the Madhyades (Central India). These Ranas of Chitor were regarded as the heads of the Rajputs. They led their armies in every direction. Malwa and Guzerat could scarcely cope with them. The Kings of

Delhi were constantly at war with them; but on the fall of Rana Sangram Singh at Sikri fighting against Babar, the Ranas lost much of their power. Bahadur Shah destroyed their capital, but was punished by Humayun. After Humayun's fall, he again invested Chitor and destroyed the city. The Emperor Akbar invested it twice, and almost annihilated the power of the Mewar kings. They then founded a city, the modern Udaipur, in the most inaccessible part of their country, and made it their capital. The Muhammadans could never penetrate to Udaipur, and the Ranas remained independent down to the period of the establishment of British supremacy.

Bengal Independent.—Bengal became independent in 1345, but its independence was disputed by Emperor Firoz Tughlak up to the year 1355. The first dynasty ruled for about half a century, and was then supplanted by Raja Ganes. His family also ruled for nearly half a century, but its second king embraced Muhammadanism and assumed the title of Jelaluddin. The first dynasty, that of Ilias Shah, was then restored, and ruled for some time. The kings were, as a rule, weak and profligate. They were completely in the hands of the Khaujas and Habsis, the guards of their household. These at last did away with the dynasty, and several of themselves ruled in succession. Alauddin Husain Shah put them down and founded a dynasty that ruled over a fairly compact territory. He made war on Orissa, Assam, and Kamatpur, which comprised modern Kuch Behar and the greater portion of Rangpur and Dinajpur. He destroyed this kingdom, and annexed most of its territory. The third in succession after Alauddin Husain Shah was expelled from Bengal by the great Sher Shah, whose descendants and relatives ruled Bengal, conquered Orissa, and were the last of the Pathan rulers of Eastern India.

The Saiyyads, 1414–1450.—After the death of Mahmud Tughlak no one assumed the imperial title. We have already said that he had discontinued coining money, and left off every other exercise of the prerogative of royalty. The kings of the next dynasty which ruled at Delhi, that of the Saiyyads, were very weak. They called themselves viceroys of Timur. They lost the Punjab, and the Lodis, who took it from them, were their perpetual enemies. They were pious men; the last of them abdicated, and retired to his garden at Badaon, and, as befitted a descendant of the Prophet, passed his remaining days in the contemplation of God.

The House of Lodi, 1450–1526.—The Lodis succeeded the Saiyyads, and thus in addition to the Punjab they became masters of the territory of Delhi. They conquered Jaunpur, and were strong rulers. The last of them, Ibrahim Lodi, was very haughty, and treated his ministers and even his generals with great disdain. His nobles, unable to bear the indignities heaped upon them, called in Babar, then king of Kabul, who conquered the Punjab and annexed it to his dominions. He then invaded the cradle of the Lodi kingdom, the province of Delhi, and defeated Ibrahim Lodi at the great battle of Panipat in 1526. Babar then assumed the title of Badshah or Emperor.

War with Sangram Singh.—The battle of Panipat gave Babar the possession of Delhi and Jaunpur. He was already master of Kabul and the Punjab. He made Delhi his capital. The establishment at Delhi of the court of a monarch who had such extensive territories, and who in addition had prestige derived from being a descendant of Timur, roused the jealousy of Rana Sangram Singh, who on a very slight pretext made war on him. The armies met at Sikri (1527) near Agra. Both sides made immense preparation. The Rajputs were confident of victory. Sangram Singh, the Rajput commander, is said to have gained no fewer than sixteen victories over the Muhammadans. But Babar was not a man to be daunted. He had risen to the imperial dignity after many trials and changes of fortune. He risked his fortune once more. In the battle that followed at Fatehpur, near Agra, both sides fought with great heroism. Victory, however, declared for the Muhammadans, and the Rajputs were routed with great slaughter.

Conquest of Malwa.—Babar followed up his success and laid siege to Chanderi, the capital of Medini Ray, the virtual dictator of Malwa. The place fell into his hands, and the fame of Babar's generalship spread far and wide. For the next two years Babar and his son, Humayun, were engaged in quelling rebellions headed by turbulent Pathan chiefs in Jaunpur, and in regulating the internal administration of the newly-acquired provinces.

Babar's Vow.—In 1530, Babar and Humayun fell seriously ill. In accordance with the popular superstition of the time, Babar made up his mind to devote his life for that of his son. He thrice turned round the bed of his dying son; and fervently muttering some prayer to God, exclaimed, "I have borne it away, I have borne it away!" This produced such a deep impression both on his own mind and on his son's that the one began to decline and the other to recover. Babar died in 1530.

Humayun Emperor.—Humayun now ascended the throne of Delhi. His brother, Kamran, was governor of Kabul and Kandahar; Humayun added the Punjab to those two provinces. Humayun's wars with Guzerat have been already described, but the great opponent of Humayun was Sher Khan, the governor of Bengal.

War with Sher Khan.—Sher Khan was the son of a Jagirdar in Behar, but was educated at Jaunpur. He was a scholar, a poet, and a critic. The troubles of the Pathans after the fall of Jaunpur induced him to become a soldier. After various changes of fortune he became the virtual ruler of Behar, and determined to conquer Bengal. Taking advantage of the weakness of the Husain Shahi dynasty he invaded Bengal, captured Gaur, and in the course of two years made a complete revenue settlement of the kingdom. Humayun came to the rescue of the dethroned king of Bengal. Though at first successful, he was twice defeated in great battles by Sher Shah and had to fly to Persia for his life. Sher Shah then made himself master of Agra, Delhi, and the Punjab.

Sher Khan ascended the throne and assumed the title of

Shah. He reigned for five years, the greater part of which was spent in improving the administration, and reducing the hill forts of the Rajputs. He first introduced a system of post-horses, constructed a highway from Gaur in Bengal to Rotas in the Punjab, and planted it on both sides with trees, excavated wells, and constructed *serais* or lodging-places for travellers at convenient distances. In 1545, he was besieging the rock fortress of Kalanjara. A shell from the fort fell into

Humayun's Tomb

his magazine, causing a terrible explosion. Sher Shah was severely scorched by the explosion, and died from the injuries. He was the greatest and wisest of the Pathan rulers of India.

Himu.—The Pathans nominally ruled for ten years more. But the great figure during these years was Himu, a deformed and ugly-looking Hindu, who from a *bazarchaudhuri* (superintendent of a market) rose to be the dictator of the Pathan empire. He was a man of uncommon ability, and combined administrative power of a high order with real military genius. The empire was seething with rebellion. Everywhere he suppressed revolts and reduced the country to order. While he was busily engaged in the east, Humayun, who had made himself master of Kabul, came back to Delhi, and occupied it after some resistance. He brought with him his famous son Akbar, the real founder of the Mughal Empire. Akbar was born in 1542, during his father's exile in the fortress of Umarkot in Sind. Himu hastened from the east, but before he reached Delhi, Humayun was dead.

Akbar's Victory at Panipat, 1556.—A great battle was fought at Panipat between Humayun's young son, Akbar, and Himu. Himu was defeated and captured. When brought before Akbar, the latter's nobles urged him to kill the infidel and to assume the title of Ghazi. Akbar was reluctant to kill a brave general and an able statesman like Himu, but Bairam Khan, Akbar's guardian, smote Himu with his sword and beheaded him.

CHAPTER VII

STATE OF INDIA UNDER THE PATHANS

The Pathan Rulers.—The Pathan empire of Delhi began to decline from the time of Muhammad Tughlak, and in fifty years was completely destroyed. Out of its ruins arose a number of independent Muhammadan kingdoms. The Pathan emperors held India by something like military occupation. They took possession of the great cities, established colonies either of Afghan tribes or of foreign mercenaries, and left the rest of the country to govern itself. They collected taxes from the tracts of country held immediately under them, and levied tribute from the Hindu Rajas who acknowledged their supremacy; but they seldom interfered in social, religious, or municipal matters, which the Hindus were allowed to manage in their own way. The Pathans checked the risings of the Hindus and protected the country from foreign invasion, but passed the rest of their time in the pursuit of pleasure.

Musalman Rulers mix with Hindus.—With the establishment of the small kingdoms a change took place. The Musalman rulers were compelled by the necessities of the position to mix with the Hindus, and to entrust them with offices of responsibility in the state. Where the influence of the Mollahs was strong, as in Guzerat, the Hindus were often persecuted, their temples destroyed, and their pilgrimages prohibited. It is said that the various places of pilgrimage in Northern India disappeared under the Muhammadan rule. This was the case with nearly all of them except Benares and Puri. Kurukshetra, Prabhas, Vrindavan, and Ajodhya had to be re-established as places of pilgrimage in the sixteenth century. The persecution of the Hindus, however, did not result in their wholesale conversion even in Muhammadan territories.

Hindu Books.—Though deprived of political power the Brahmans kept the Hindu society intact by the compilation of a large number of works recording minutely the laws and the religious and social observances required from Hindus by their religion. These assumed the position of the highest authority in the Hindu society, and had learned Brahmans for their interpreters, such a position, in fact, as Raghunandan's works at present hold in Bengal.

Hindu Reforms.—During the Pathan period Hindu society underwent another great revolution. Great reformers (such as Nanak, and Chaitanya) appeared in the various provinces of India, preaching faith and devotion as superior to rituals and asceticism. As in the fifth and sixth centuries before the Christian era, so in the fifteenth and sixteenth centuries after it, the reformers persuaded men to renounce the world. Thus the Hindu community was again split up into bodies opposed to each other, and obeying as their religious guides two distinct classes of teachers, the Brahmans and the mendicants. Like the Buddhists and the Jains of the earlier period, the later reformers made the several vernaculars the medium of communication with the people, and raised many of the dialects to the dignity of literary languages. The followers of Chaitanya improved Bengali; those of Nanak, Punjabi.

CHAPTER VIII

AKBAR

Akbar's Birth.—While flying before Sher Shah, Humayun accepted the hospitality of the petty Rajput chief of Umarkot, in the desert bordering on Sind. His favourite *begum* was in the family way and had suffered from the privations of a hurried journey through the desert. Here at Umarkot she gave birth to a child. It is customary in the East to distribute presents among friends on such an auspicious occasion. Humayun had only a pod of musk with him. This he opened and distributed among his friends, saying that the fame of the new-born child would spread far and wide like the fragrance of this musk. Never was a father's prediction more literally fulfilled.

Bairam Khan.—Akbar came to the throne when he was only fourteen. Nominally he was ruler of all the territories from the west of Kabul to the east of Bengal; but, practically, he was the weakest of monarchs. He was surrounded by ambitious adventurers ready to carve out kingdoms for themselves, and his subjects had no loyalty to his house. He had only one faithful servant, his guardian Bairam Khan, who for four years actually ruled the kingdom of Delhi with an iron hand. He took the title of Khan Baba, and acted as Regent till Akbar came of age. He did much that was wrong, but did it all in the interests of his ward. He was overbearing and harsh, and made many enemies for himself. After Akbar assumed the government, Bairam was setting out on a pilgrimage when he was murdered by an Afghan whose father he had killed in battle. At eighteen Akbar assumed the sovereignty, but it took him seven years to bring his subordinates under control and to firmly establish his own power. Then began a career of conquest unique in the history of the Muhammadans in India.

Character of Akbar's Conquests.—Akbar's conquests were not like those of Alauddin; they were not merely cases of overrunning the various countries and holding them temporarily in military occupation. They were real conquests. The people were conciliated, and settled governments everywhere established, the rulers acknowledging their dependence on Akbar. His first conquest was that of Malwa, the ruler of which, the flighty Baj Bahadur, so famous in Malwa legends, accepted service under the emperor, and was employed by him in distant conquests. The king of Kashmir, after the conquest of that countrv by Akbar, accepted jagirs in Behar.

Mausoleum of Akbar

The king of Guzerat was one of the leading figures at Akbar's court. The sultan of Sind was treated by the emperor with equal courtesy and consideration.

Struggle with Pathans of Bengal.—In two quarters in Northern India Akbar met with stubborn resistance. The Pathans, gradually ousted from the rest of India, found a stronghold in Bengal, then ruled by the descendants of the conqueror of Orissa. They were jealous of Akbar's growing powers and made war upon him. Akbar's Muhammadan generals defeated them and broke their power; but later, rebelling against the emperor, joined the Pathans and gave Akbar much trouble. From these troubles he was relieved by two Rajput nobles, whom his conciliatory policy had attached to his person and court. One of these was Man Singh, Raja of Jaipur, whose sister Akbar had married, and the other was Todar Mall. Man Singh was twice sent to Bengal as governor. In his first administration he restrained the Mughal nobles and compelled the Pathans to settle in Orissa. Todar Mall made the revenue settlement of Bengal, fixing the total rent at one-third of the produce. The second administration of Man Singh was occupied with the subjugation of Pratapaditya, Raja of Jessore.

Struggle with Rajputs of Mewar.—Akbar met with even fiercer opposition from the Rajputs of Mewar. He, however, broke their power; brought many of their subordinate chiefs to his court, and won them over to his side by granting them high offices. He annexed much of the Rajput territory and destroyed Chitor, their capital; but the spirit of the Rajputs was not broken. They disdained to mix their high caste blood even with that of an emperor. After wanderings in the mountains and deserts, the Raja established his capital at Udaipur, in an inaccessible part of the country where the Mughals could never penetrate, and continued to rule independently even after the fall of the Mughal empire.

Internal Quarrels among Musalmans of Deccan.—After the assassination of Mahmud Gawan, the opposing elements which his genius kept in check came into conflict. This resulted in the dismemberment of the Bahamani kingdoms. The two opposing elements which the genius of Mahmud restrained were the Deccani Musalmans and the foreign Musalmans. Five kingdoms were formed out of the ruins of the Bahamani dominions. The foreign Musalmans established the kingdoms of Bijapur and Golconda, and supplanted the Bahamanis at Bidar. The Hindu converts to Muhammadanism established themselves at Ahmadnagar and Berar. But in a short time even in these five states two fiercely antagonistic parties appeared, one of foreign and the other of Deccani Musalmans, so that there was perpetual disquiet and unrest everywhere. Bidar soon became united with Bijapur and Berar with Ahmadnagar. Golconda entered upon a career of conquest of the Hindu principalities south of the Krishna. Once only the Musalmans acted in concert. When the Hindus of Vijayanagar insulted the king of Ahmadnagar and heaped indignities on his subjects, they combined to punish the offenders. After the battle of Talikot and the fall of Vijayanagar, however, their mutual jealousies prevented their profiting by their victories. A short time afterwards Ahmadnagar was embroiled in a quarrel with Akbar.

Akbar's Conquests in Deccan.—In the first expedition Akbar took the Berars from Ahmadnagar and Bidar from Bijapur. Then there was a lull in the strife. During this Chand Sultana, a princess of Ahmadnagar, the widow of a king of Bijapur, reorganized the government of Ahmadnagar and put the Musalman affairs on a better footing. Thereupon her opponents, the leaders of the Deccani party, invited Akbar to take possession of Ahmadnagar. The Mughals laid siege to the city, Chand Sultana was assassinated, and the town fell into the hands of the besiegers. Chand Sultana's party established another capital known at present as Arangabad, and continued the resistance till they were finally conquered by Shah Jahan. Thus at the time of his death Akbar was master of nearly three of the five Deccani kingdoms.

Character of Akbar.—Akbar made many conquests, but he was never fond of war. When once war was forced upon him, however, he was all energy and perseverance. He superintended all the preparations, and often took the command in the beginning of the campaign. He was a fast rider and a tireless pedestrian. In time of need he would swim across rivers swollen by the rains. He divided India into fifteen subahs or provinces, each presided over by a Nazim or governor assisted by a Dewan or finance minister. The dewan received his appointment from the emperor, and was in no way subordinate to the nazim. The other appointments were left to the nazim. His generals received jagirs, but his troops were always paid from the imperial treasury. The generals had their different grades. There were commanders of five thousand, commanders of seven thousand, and so on. The highest commands were reserved for the royal princes. Even these, however, were sometimes given to generals who had rendered signal service to the state. Man Sinha obtained such a high command.

His Patronage of Learning.—Akbar was not a learned man. In all literary matters he depended upon two great scholars. One of these was Faizi, the first Muhammadan Sanskrit scholar, and the other was Abul Fazl, the great historian of Akbar's reign. Long peace and good government made it possible for a vernacular literature to spring up and flourish in the various provinces of the empire; and it is a curious fact that Sanskrit literature also flourished at this time. A historian, not very well affected towards Akbar, says, with a whine, that no one could obtain preferment or promotion unless he translated some Sanskrit work into Persian. The translators in Akbar's reign of the Ramayana and the Mahabharata were governors of provinces.

Akbar's Religious Attitude.—Akbar was fond of associating with the great doctors of the various religions taught in his dominions. He used to call meetings of these teachers at his court, and listen attentively to their discourses. Hindus, Musalmans, Jains, Christians of various shades of opinion, figured at these meetings. After long deliberation Akbar came to the conclusion that God is one, and that the sun is his visible emblem in the universe. With this as the cardinal doctrine of his faith, he founded a religion known as the *Ilahi* religion. Akbar did away with the old forms of greeting. For Salam-al-ekam he substituted "Alla-ho-Akbar" (God is great). The formula in reply to this was "Zilli-Zillali-ho" (He is the brightest of the bright). He did not like long beards, and he compelled all his nobles to shave. This gave great offence to the Mollahs, who thought that wearing beards was obligatory on Musalmans.

CHAPTER IX

AKBAR'S IMMEDIATE SUCCESSORS

Jahangir, 1605–1627.—The successor of Akbar was not a man of steady habits. He had given much trouble during his father's reign; and on one occasion he even rebelled against him. He caused Abul Fazl, his father's friend, the philosopher and historian, to be assassinated by a Rajput chief of Bundelkhand. Abul Fazl was so great a favourite of Akbar, that when the news of his murder reached the emperor, he wept bitterly, and took no food or drink for two days.

His Love of Justice.—On coming to the throne Jahangir showed great solicitude for the better administration of justice. He is said to have suspended a rope outside his palace connecting it with a bell inside. Anyone demanding justice could pull the rope and inform the emperor that he was a suitor, and he got instant audience. There were wars in his reign not worth much notice. He married a beautiful widow, who became famous as Nur Jahan, or the Light of the World. Her enchanting eyes, clear-cut features, long and slender neck, and rosy complexion made her really one of the most famous beauties the world has seen. Some of Jahangir's troubles arose from his excessive fondness for Nur Jahan. But she was a noble woman, and helped her husband greatly in his management of the affairs of his empire, and her name was associated with his in all public documents, and was inscribed on the coins issued.

Prohibited Use of Tobacco.—Jahangir, though fond of strong drink, prohibited the use of tobacco, then recently introduced into India by the Portuguese, who brought it from the island of Tobago in America.

Shah Jahan, 1628–1658.—On her husband's death, Nur Jahan, with the help of the relatives, whom during his life she had advanced in power, tried to raise her son-in-law, one of the sons of Jahangir by another of his queens, to the throne; but Shah Jahan defeated her, killed her son-in-law, murdered his own brothers and kinsmen, and pensioned off Nur Jahan. He had great trouble with Khan Jahan Lodi, one of his generals who rebelled against him, collected together his Afghan tribesmen, joined the party of independence at Ahmadnagar, and after ten years of hopeless struggle escaped to Afghanistan.

Character of Shah Jahan.—Shah Jahan was a good man and a good king. Whatever his faults might have been in early youth, his character completely changed on his accession to the throne. He always behaved, both in public and in private, in a manner befitting the emperor of Hindustan. Though he was prone to anger, he was an affectionate father, a warm friend, and a loving husband. He placed entire confidence in his sons—a thing which in the end proved his ruin.

The Tajmahal.—The death of his wife, Mum Tajmahal, moved him greatly, and he built a mausoleum over her remains at an immense cost. This is the celebrated Tajmahal, one of the wonders of the world. It stands on the Jumna, at a short distance from the palace at Agra, from which it looks like a picture, and it has been described by competent critics as a sigh in marble. Shah Jahan lies buried in the Tajmahal by the side of his beloved empress. Often in his misery he sat in the veranda of the palace overlooking the Jumna gazing at the spot where the remains of all that he loved on earth lay buried.

Mir Jumla, and the King of Golconda.—Mir Jumla was a small trader when he came to India. He settled at Golconda, and worked the mines. He found many diamonds, and attracted the notice of the king of Golconda, who employed him in the public service; and he gradually rose to the highest position in the state. He was employed in the conquest of the petty Hindu principalities in the south, which defied the power of the king of Golconda for many years. His great success made the king jealous, and he plotted to have him assassinated. Mir Jumla discovered this, and fled to the Mughal camp, and wrote a letter to Shah Jahan, stating his case and offering his allegiance. Shah Jahan was very angry; and ordered his third son, the viceroy of the Deccan, to annex the kingdoms of Bijapur and Golconda to the Mughal empire. Ahmadnagar had been finally conquered by Shah Jahan some years before. The kingdoms of Bijapur and Golconda would soon have been destroyed but for an unfortunate and unforeseen event.

The Struggles for Dominion.—The details of the Hindu administration are not yet known; but from what we read in the smritis, in the works on politics, and in the poems and dramas, it is apparent that the kings often had great trouble with their sons or other would-be successors. During the Pathan period kings often died by the hands of their sons who wished to succeed them, or by the hands of would-be usurpers. The Mughal government was generally conducted on more civilized principles; but on the death of every emperor there was a civil war among his sons; and if he did not leave behind more than one son, between his son and his grandson. At Akbar's death Jahangir had to face a serious opposition, for some of his nobles wanted to place his son, Khusru, on the throne. Shah Jahan was more unfortunate still. He was a loving father, and he advanced all his sons to positions of power.

Revolt of Shah Jahan's Sons.—On hearing that their father was seriously ill, all of his four sons prepared for a struggle for the succession. His eldest son, Dara, was his favourite, and remained with him at Agra looking after the administration of the empire. His second son, Shuja, was subahdar of Bengal; the third, Aurangzeb, was the subahdar of the Deccan; and the fourth, Murad, of Guzerat. Aurangzeb knew how to conceal his plans. Mir Jumla was with him, and was ready to help him with his immense wealth. He affected to be reluctant to begin a civil war; and he allowed Mir Jumla to think that only his advice and entreaties led him to take such a bold step. He easily lulled the suspicions of Murad, and induced that foolish and impulsive prince to join him, by representing that his endeavours were directed against the infidel Dara, and that as soon as that prince was defeated and punished, he himself would place Murad on the throne and then retire to Mecca.

Aurangzeb's Treachery.—Aurangzeb had all the Musalmans with him, and Dara's principal supporters were the Rajput princes. Dara was twice defeated, and had to flee for life. He was, however, brought back and beheaded as an infidel and an apostate. Shuja was twice defeated, and compelled to take refuge with the king of Arakan. What became of him is not known. Too late Murad learned that he had been deceived. He was sent to the fort of Gwalior, and compelled there to drink every morning a cup of *post*, a narcotic liquor prepared from poppy-heads, by boiling these in water with unrefined palm-sugar, so that he became weak and imbecile in a short time. He lingered on for some time, and then died unknown and uncared for. Such was the fate which the emperors of Delhi decreed for those who had the remotest chance of setting themselves up as their rivals.

Death of Shah Jahan.—Shah Jahan rallied from his illness, and protested against the conduct of his children, but Aurangzeb was victorious. He deposed his father, confined him in an apartment of the palace, waited for a year to dispose of the affairs of his brothers; and when they had all been got rid of, declared himself emperor.

CHAPTER X

AURANGZEB, 1658–1707

Treatment of Supporters. — The first care of the new emperor, after getting rid of his father and his brothers, was to get rid of the friends of whom he was jealous. He sent Mir Jumla to Bengal, simply to keep him away from Delhi. That ambitious upstart formed the project of invading China; was embroiled in a vexatious quarrel with the Raja of Assam; lost his army; returned to Bengal in great affliction, and died of a broken heart. Thus Aurangzeb easily got rid of the friend he distrusted.

Reimposition of Jazia.—As a conscientious Muhammadan ruler Aurangzeb could not help reimposing on his non-Musalman subjects the *Jazia*, a poll-tax enjoined in the Koran. Its abolition and the various other acts of conciliation of Akbar and his successors had attached the Hindus in general, and the Rajput princes in particular, to the throne of Delhi. But Aurangzeb was a staunch Musalman, and his attitude towards the Hindus was far from conciliatory. Naturally they were dissatisfied. They said that a change had come over the attitude of the rulers towards them. They were indignant at the reimposition of the hated poll-tax. They protested. Crowds waited on the emperor with petitions against the tax. In the streets of Delhi such petitions were presented to him as he proceeded on his elephant to the Juma Musjid or principal mosque. He turned a deaf ear to these prayers of his Hindu subjects. They besought him to listen to them. On their knees they implored him to take pity on them, but he remained obdurate. He ordered the crowds to disperse. They continued to beseech him to have mercy, till at last he ordered his elephant-driver to proceed. Crowds were trampled under the elephant's feet, but the emperor was not moved. His heart did not melt at the sufferings of his subjects. He held to his scheme, and continued to levy the poll-tax. The Hindus were driven from the administration, and their wrongs forced some of them into rebellion.

War with Rajputs.—The petitions of the Hindu citizens of Delhi, the representations of the Hindu subjects of the empire might be despised, but not so the protests of the Rajput princes. At first they protested in vain; then they flew to arms. Aurangzeb ill-treated the family of Yasovant Sinha, the Raja of Marwar and the subahdar of Kabul, a faithful servant of the empire. Raja Raj Sinha of Mewar headed the Rajput movement. The statesmanship and the heroism displayed by Raj Sinha during this struggle excites the admiration even of the supporters of Aurangzeb. Aurangzeb could not subdue the Rajputs, could not break their spirit. His immense army was useless in the narrow passes of Rajputana. He suffered great reverses; and, to secure a temporary peace, he had to submit to humiliating terms.

The Emperor's Ambition.—The great object of the emperor's ambition was universal empire in India, and he was anxious to annex Golconda and Bijapur. But he could not leave the capital when the Rajputs were in arms at his door, so he had to patch up a peace with them before he proceeded to the Deccan. It took no great length of time to conquer these two Muhammadan kingdoms, propped up though they were by the skill and diplomacy of Hindus like Shahji and Morad Panth. Both kingdoms were rent in pieces by the jealousies of their ambitious Musalman nobles. Aurangzeb's generals proceeded after the conquest of Bijapur and Golconda to overrun the small kingdom south of Krishna, which had been quietly developing the arts of peace and war since the fall of Vijayanagar.

Opposition of Hindus.—Aurangzeb's dream of universal empire in India seemed about to be realized. There was, however, one serious drawback. A change had come over the spirit of the Hindus of the Deccan during the period intervening between Aurangzeb's viceroyalty of the Deccan and his march into the country as emperor. A Hindu kingdom had been founded on the borders of Ahmadnagar and Bijapur by Sivaji, the son of a Marhatta Jagirdar, or possessor of the right to a jagir, that is, to govern and levy taxes on a district. But this kingdom could not resist the army of Aurangzeb led by himself; and its Raja, Sambhaji, was captured and put to death. The capital of the Marhattas was seized, and the new Raja, the infant son of Sambhaji, taken prisoner. Apparently Aurangzeb was the emperor of all India. There remained only the Marhatta dacoits to suppress. These were nothing more than dacoits. They had no kingdom, no fort, no capital, and no king. Only they were rather a bold set of dacoits, still they were dacoits for all that. With the dream of empire over all India thus seemingly realized, Aurangzeb breathed his last in 1707 A.D.

Character of Aurangzeb.—Aurangzeb was extremely suspicious. He suspected that the Hindus might one day overthrow the Muhammadan power. He suspected that the Muhammadans, as they were ambitious, turbulent, and self-seeking, might one day overthrow his house. He was suspicious of his sons, who, he often thought, with his own example before their eyes, might reduce him one day to the condition of Shah Jahan, or perhaps to a worse condition. He trusted nobody. He always had checks and counterchecks on his officers, and his spies were everywhere throughout the empire. That such a suspicious man ruled over an empire for nearly fifty years speaks well for the solidarity of the empire founded by Akbar. One of the consequences of this inability to trust others was that the emperor had to look minutely into every department of state. It says much for his aptitude for work that he continued personally to supervise everything, even to so advanced an age as ninety-one. The Muhammadans extol him to the skies, because he contrasts so favourably in their eyes with his predecessors; and it must be confessed that the simplicity of his habits, and his diligence and business capacity, entitle him to a respect hard to reconcile with the murder of his brothers, the deposition of his father, and the persecution of his Hindu subjects.

CHAPTER XI

FALL OF THE MUGHAL EMPIRE

Aurangzeb's Successors.—Aurangzeb's successors were all weak men. As he suspected all his sons and grandsons of possibly entertaining designs to dethrone him, he did not give them an education befitting their high position. He watched them all narrowly; and they never had any free scope for exercising their powers. Consequently after Aurangzeb's death the ambitious nobles kept them under tutelage and set up and pulled down emperors at their pleasure.

The Actual Rulers.—For the first few years Zulfikar Khan was the greatest figure at Delhi, overshadowing even the emperor himself. For the second period the Sayyid brothers, Husain Ali and Abdulla, ruled the emperor and the empire as well. During the third period the dismemberment of the empire began. The six subahs or provinces of the Deccan slipped from the feeble hands of the emperor. They were seized by a refractory nobleman, who, invested with the title of Nizam-ul-mulk or governor of the Deccan, established his independence, and cut off the greater part of Southern India from the empire. Kabul was occupied by the Persians. Malwa and Guzerat were conquered by the Marhattas, and the emperor granted them *sanads* as subahdars or lords of the provinces. The subahdars of Bengal and Oudh acted independently for some time, and then withheld the revenue. The name, the external form, and the prestige of the empire remained, but its power was gone.

The Marhatta and Persian Invasions.—Then came successive invasions from west and south, which destroyed the last vestiges of the power of the emperors of Delhi. The first of these invasions was led by the great Marhatta chief, Baji Rao Peshwa, who plundered the country up to the very gates of Delhi. The second was led by the impetuous Nadir Shah, who from the position of a cowherd on the banks of the Caspian rose to be the emperor of Persia, comprehending under his dominion Afghanistan, the greater part of Turkey, and much of what is now known as Russia. His name was a terror at Constantinople, at St. Petersburg, and even at Vienna. He came to India, 1739; plundered the treasury at Delhi; compelled every street of Delhi to raise a fixed sum of money; collected tributes from the various provinces of India; took away the peacock throne and the Kohinur; and, provoked by the jeers of the citizens, ordered a general massacre. He, however, treated the emperor of Delhi with the greatest kindness and courtesy, and ordered the Indian nobles to obey his brother, Mahamad Shah, emperor of Delhi, threatening them with heavy penalties if they failed to do so. It is calculated that the treasure carried off by Nadir Shah exceeded in value thirty millions sterling.

Afghan Invasion.—The third invasion was by Ahmad Shah Abdalli, who founded a compact kingdom in Afghanistan on the ruins of Nadir's empire, interfered in the affairs of the Punjab, and though once compelled to retreat, finally occupied and sacked Delhi. The fourth invasion was by the Marhattas, who brought down the silver ceiling of the *am-khash*, and plundered the whole country up to the banks of the Indus, and talked of a Hindu Empire.

Nominal Supremacy of the Emperor of Delhi.—No empire can last under such repeated shocks. The Mughal Empire was altogether broken, but still the emperor of Delhi was regarded as the emperor of India. His *sanads* or patents were sought for by the most powerful. Money was coined in his name, and he held nominally the highest place in India; but his power hardly extended otherwise beyond the walls of his palace.

CHAPTER XII

CAUSES OF FALL OF MUGHAL EMPIRE

Conciliatory Attitude of Early Mughals to Hindus.—During the period between the fall of the Pathans and the rise of the Mughals, a friendly intercourse seems to have sprung up between the Hindus and their conquerors. The fierce spirit of proselytism, which characterized the Muhammadans during the Imperial Pathan period, the spirit to which we owe the conversion of nearly a third of Bengal, half the Rajput races, the greater part of Kasmir, and vast tracts in Malwa, Guzerat, and the Deccan, had, to a great extent, abated. Intermarriage with the Hindus, and their employment in the higher offices of the state and as military leaders, as well as the adoption of various Hindu customs by numerous Muhammadan families, marked what seemed the beginning of an amalgamation of the races, or, at least, of mutual toleration.

Akbar's Toleration.—Akbar, with a profound insight into human character, adopted a policy which emphasized this spirit of toleration between the races that had already sprung up in the course of the previous centuries. Friendly intercourse increased. The Muhammadans began to respect learned Brahmans and Sannyasis (ascetics or Hindu mendicants), while the Hindus also had recourse for spiritual instruction to Muhammadan Pirs (saints) and Fakirs (mendicants). The thrifty Hindus began to grow in wealth and power, and became an element of strength in the Mughal empire. The small Hindu principalities, which still retained their independence, shared in the general prosperity of their co-religionists, and it often happened that these independent chiefs accepted military service under the emperor. If the policy adopted by Akbar had continued to be the accepted policy, the destiny of India would have been very different.

Aurangzeb's Persecution.—But circumstances forced Aurangzeb to adopt a pronounced Muhammadan policy, which estranged the feelings, not only of his Hindu subjects, but also of the friendly Hindu chiefs. The Rajputs revolted. The Jats created disturbances in the immediate vicinity of the capital. The Sikhs, unable to bear a most inhuman persecution, took a religious vow to avenge themselves on their persecutors. The wild tribes everywhere made common cause with the Hindus, and the Marhattas determined not only to establish an independent kingdom in the Muhammadan territories, but to sap the very foundation of the Mughal empire by carrying violence and rapine from one end of the country to the other.

CHAPTER XIII

INDEPENDENT STATES

Small Hindu Kingdoms.—Though the Marhatta country was early annexed to the Muhammadan empire, yet there were many small independent Hindu kings who reigned in the Sahyadri (Western Ghats) and in the Konkan (the country between the Western Ghats and the sea). It took two centuries and the genius of a Mahmud Gawan to subdue them. Even then the collection of revenues remained entirely in the hands of the Hindus. Every village was under the charge of a revenue officer named *Gramadhikari*, and every district under a *Desamukhya*, who received a tenth of the revenue as *sardesmukhi*, or the dues of a desamukhya. After the fall of the Bahmani dynasty, the Hindu desamukhyas in Maharashtra became subordinate to either Bijapur or Ahmadnagar. They used to collect revenue, garrison hill forts, and, in time of war, to fight under the standard of some Muhammadan general. Many of the desamukhyas obtained extensive jagirs or grants of the right to collect state revenues for distinguished services. Of these, seven large Marhatta jagirdars, or holders of such rights, served the Bijapur and two the Ahmadnagar state. The Yadavas of Sindhekir were allied by marriage to that of the Bhonslas; and as both the families served under the Ahmadnagar state, a friendly feeling always subsisted between them. Shahji Bhonsla was married to the daughter of Lukhji Yadava Ray, and Sivaji, the founder of the Marhatta power, was born of this marriage.

Rise of Sivaji.—Sivaji was early left in charge of his father's jagir of Poona. He reclaimed the wild tribes of Mawalis (the mountain valleys in the Sahyadri) and trained them as soldiers. He was an out-and-out Hindu, and listened to the stories of the Ramayana and the Mahabharata with great attention. He was early fired with the ambition of founding an independent Hindu kingdom and of getting rid of Muhammadan supremacy. With this view he not only reclaimed the Mawalis but collected troops, arms, and ammunition. He began his career by plunder, the proceeds of which he carefully employed in increasing his military strength. He had no hill forts in which he could keep the treasures he had captured. He built one, seized one by treachery, and took possession of a third, the owners of which had quarrelled among themselves and submitted to his arbitration. He secured a fourth belonging to the Bijapur state, and represented to the king that it was the interest of the state that the fort should be in the hands of a faithful servant like himself. He plundered the convoys of treasure, first those of Bijapur and then those of the Mughals.

He plundered the seaports of Surat and Vasava. He destroyed the power of the Ghorepures and annexed their jagir to his own. He often made war on Bijapur and even on the Mughals.

Treatment of Sivaji by Emperor.—Aurangzeb was greatly annoyed with Sivaji because he plundered the pilgrim ships on the way to Mecca. He sent some of his best generals against him, but the Marhatta always baffled them. He was, however, induced by one of the Rajput generals to proceed to Delhi and to cultivate friendly relations with Aurangzeb, the general standing as a security for his life. Aurangzeb had an excellent opportunity of converting a dangerous enemy into a fast friend. But he was the model of a Muhammadan king, and so he treated the infidel Sivaji with studied disrespect. Sivaji, who had already declared himself independent and assumed the title of Raja, was given a seat with noblemen of the third class at the Delhi court. He was greatly annoyed, and returned to his residence only to find that he was a prisoner.

Escape from Delhi.—Attempts were made on his life, but the Rajput general who brought Sivaji to Delhi reminded the emperor that he stood security for Sivaji's life. In a short time, however, the wily Marhatta formed a plan of escape which no Muhammadan was at all likely to suspect. On a full-moon day he distributed basketfuls of sweetmeats to the Brahmans of Delhi. Many baskets were despatched from his residence, and when suspicion was completely lulled he entered one of the covered baskets and thereby escaped from Delhi.

Sivaji establishes an Independent Kingdom.—Sivaji was already full of hatred for the Muhammadans. His journey to Delhi only served to intensify that feeling and to add to his resolution to break down the Muhammadan power. By incessant efforts he soon made himself master of a mountainous territory, two hundred miles long and one hundred broad. He was also master of the whole of the Konkan coast with the exception of Goa, Bombay, and Jinjira. He sent for the greatest Marhatta Pundits from Benares, and had himself crowned according to the coronation rites of the ancient Kshatriyas. He began to coin money in his own name, and assumed all the insignia of royalty. He formed a privy-council of eight members. These were heads of the eight departments of state. The Peshwa was at the head of this council. The king himself presided at its meetings.

Conquest of his Kingdom by Emperor.—Sivaji died at the age of fifty-one. The territory acquired by him goes in the Marhatta records by the name of Svarajya. This kingdom was, however, completely destroyed by Aurangzeb within twenty years of Sivaji's death.

On Aurangzeb's death the king of the Marhattas, Sahu, the

Satara

son of Sambhaji, who had been detained in the emperor's camp, was released, and he soon managed to get possession of the entire territory; but he was compelled to surrender a part of his kingdom to another grandson of Sivaji, whose descendants are still ruling at Kolapur. The new king established his capital at Satara, and was nominally the head of the Marhattas.

Claim to Chauth and Sardesmukhi.—Besides the Svarajya Sivaji laid claim to a fourth of the revenue (*chauth*) of all the subahs of the Deccan, on condition that he would never trouble any subahdar who would pay him this tribute regularly. This claim was often allowed by the subahdars and often enforced by Sivaji at the head of an army. This formed an integral part of his revenue and used to be deposited in the treasury.

He claimed another impost called the *sardesmukhi* (the tenth of the revenue), which he claimed as the Desamukhya. This formed his personal income.

The Plundering by the Marhattas.—During the twenty-six years which Aurangzeb outlived Sivaji the Marhatta kingdom seemed completely broken; but the great officers of the Marhatta state never ceased plundering the Mughal territories. Later their armies were strengthened by the disbanded soldiery of Bijapur and Golconda. One of the Marhatta senapatis or generals established a dominion for himself at Gooti in the Madras Presidency, and another at Guzerat. A Marhatta chief settled at Nagpur, where Muhammadan power had never penetrated, and there he founded a large kingdom. Everywhere the Marhattas claimed the chauth and the sardesmukhi.

The Marhattas also claimed another impost, which they called *ghasdana* (grass and grain) or forage money, and which was used for the benefit of the plundering chiefs.

Grant of Chauth to the Marhattas.—After the release of the Marhatta king Sahu the struggle between the empire and the Marhattas continued. But the efforts on the Mughal side were languid and spasmodic, while on the side of the Marhattas they were energetic and persistent. The great nobles of Delhi found this state of things to be disadvantageous to the empire, and so they acknowledged the Marhattas to be independent in their svarajya, induced the emperor to grant a *sanad* authorizing them to levy chauth and sardesmukhi in the subahs of the Deccan, and the Marhattas agreed to help the emperor in times of need with 15,000 horse.

Their Revenue System.—The revenue system of the Marhattas after this treaty became very complicated. The only man who understood it thoroughly was Balaji Vishnath Bhatt, a Konkan Brahman of great ability and astuteness. He was therefore raised to the rank of Peshwa by Sahu, who, owing to his long confinement among the Mughals, was a rather degenerate Mahratta, and wasted his life in slothfulness, yielding up the administration of affairs to his minister.

Baji Rao.—Balaji, however, did not live long. He was

succeeded by his able son, Baji Rao, a young man of twenty, very handsome, very popular, and very accomplished. He was a genius both in civil and in military administration. From 1720 to 1740 he was the greatest figure in India. His activity knew no bounds. If Sivaji had founded a Marhatta kingdom, Baji Rao raised it to the position of an empire. He induced Sahu the king to grant him the viceroyalty of the Konkan, and the power of levying the Marhatta dues in the Deccan, Guzerat, and Malwa. This power to levy tribute he made into practically the sovereignty of Southern India. In Guzerat he came into conflict with the senapati or general who was collecting the Marhatta dues. The senapati died in the course of the war that ensued. The king Sahu, on the advice of Baji Rao, appointed the senapati's infant son to his father's place, with Pilaji Gwakwar as his guardian. This was the foundation of the greatness of the Gwakwar family, for the infant son of the senapati died early. The king permitted the guardian of the senapati and the Peshwa to jointly collect the Marhatta dues in Guzerat and to divide them equally. The Peshwa and Pilaji Gwakwar joined to conquer the territories under the Mughal subahdars, and soon became masters of Guzerat, and jointly obtained a subahdar sanad from the great Mughal.

His Conquest of Malwa.—Baji Rao plundered Malwa several times. Once he went up to Delhi. The emperor, powerless to resist, requested the subahdar of the Deccan to become his vizier. The subahdar came, assumed his new office, collected the entire strength of the Mughal empire, and proceeded to Bhopal, where Baji Rao with 80,000 horse began to harass the Mughal army. The Mughal camp was protected by artillery. Baji never came within the range of the guns, but kept the army there for months together. He cut off their supplies, made the approach of reinforcement impossible, and harassed them in every way. The subahdar vizier had to conciliate him by making him the subahdar of Malwa and giving him a large money grant from the imperial treasury. Baji Rao divided Malwa among his generals, Ranaji Scindhia,

Malhar Rao, Holkar, and Udaiji Pwar—the founders of the great houses of Gwalior, Indore, and Dhar.

Shortly before this, by aiding the Raja of Bundelkhand, Baji Rao obtained Jhansi in full sovereignty. He conquered Salset and Bassein from the Portuguese, and obtained from the Raja the viceroyalty of these important places.

The Raja of Nagpur.—The Raja of Nagpur invaded Bengal, and after ten years of plunder, compelled the subahdar to grant him Orissa in full sovereignty, and to pay him a tribute of twelve lakhs of rupees a year in lieu of the chauth for Bengal.

His Quarrel with Baji Rao.—There arose a quarrel between the Raja of Nagpore and the son of Baji Rao about the chauth of Hindustan. The Raja of Satara arbitrated. His judgment was that the Raja of Nagpur should confine himself to Bengal, Behar, and Orissa, while the rest of Northern India should be given to the Peshwa.

Balaji and his Dewan.—Baji Rao died in 1740. He was deeply in debt, contracted in furtherance of his policy, and was greatly harassed both by his creditors and by his rivals. "I should be thankful if I could meet death," he had cried in despair only a little before. His son, Balaji Baji Rao, succeeded him. Balaji's Dewan, or chief officer, advanced him money to enable him to pay off his father's debts, and Balaji gratefully made him the Dewan of the Peshwa; but a few years later Sadasiva Rao Bhao, the cousin of Balaji, claimed the office as his by hereditary right, since his father had been dewan. Balaji was in a fix. If Sadasiva did not get it, there would be serious dissensions in the family. Yet how could he take it away from one who had paid so much for it, who had been so helpful when he was in difficulties? From this dilemma he was relieved by the dewan voluntarily resigning. For this act of generosity the dewan's name is still held in great respect by the Marhatta nation.

Raghoba.—Balaji's brother, Raghoba, was a brave soldier and a skilful general. He planned and led an expedition to the banks of the Indus, seized Lahore, and forced the

Afghans to withdraw to the west of that river. Sadasiva obtained possession of the fort and district of Ahmadnagar by bribing the Mughal officer in charge. There was a war with the Nizam in consequence, and the Marhattas gained much territory.

Sadasiva and Battle of Panipat.—Sadasiva led the next Marhatta expedition to Northern India. He went, not in old Marhatta style, but in the Mughal fashion, with pomp and grandeur. But he had to face a terrible opponent in Ahmad Shah Abdali, who had under his command the forces of the provinces still nominally part of the Mughal empire. The armies met at Panipat. The Marhattas were in difficulties. They had no supplies, and no money to purchase them. They had already stripped the country of all that was available. They were compelled by famine to make an attack on Ahmad's fortified positions. The inevitable consequence of the failure of such an attack is ruinous defeat, and this was what fell to the lot of the Marhattas. Sadasiva perished, and with him 200,000 Marhatta soldiers, the flower of the nation.

Afghans and English.—The battle of Panipat gave to the Afghans a hold on Western India, while in the east the English were feeling their way to the sovereignty of Bengal, Behar, and Orissa. It would be interesting to take a rapid survey of the political condition of India at this time, as it is the period of the commencement of the British Raj.

Division of India.—In the west the Punjab was lost to Delhi. Ahmad Shah Abdali had appointed a governor of his own in that province, but his government was not at all stable. The Sikhs and Musalmans were fighting. They vied with each other in lawlessness and brutality. Sirhind, Delhi, and Agra belonged nominally to the emperor, but he was himself a wanderer in Behar, living on the charity of his subjects and of the British. The government of these subahs was in the hands of the Rohillas, the Afghan settlers of Rohilkhand. Oudh and its neighbouring subahs were in the hands of an ambitious subahdar, who acted according to what he considered his interests and inclinations, and who was anxious to make himself master of Hindustan. Benares and Allahabad were already his. The subahdar of Bengal acted independently, and remitted no revenue since the invasion of his country by the Raja of Nagpur. He was master of the three subahs of Bengal, Behar, and Orissa, but he had already made over Orissa to the Marhattas. Sind, neglected by the feeble emperor, had fallen into the hands of certain Baluch chiefs, who had parcelled out the lands among themselves. They owned no superiors. One among them was called head of the chiefs, and he had a peculiar turban, this being the distinguishing mark of his headship. The Rajputs were already feeling the dangerous proximity of the Marhattas in Malwa and Guzerat. Three important chiefs were ruling these two subahs under the headship of the ambitious Brahman house of Poona. To the east of these was the Raja of Nagpur. These four great houses were subordinate to the Peshwa, but the Peshwa could scarcely enforce obedience without the help of an army. He was no longer the head of plundering bands, but the sovereign of extensive territories, with a revenue that was reckoned in crores of rupees.

Divisions of the Deccan.—The Subahdar of the Deccan was master of six subahs, the southernmost of which acted independently of him. Mysore was a big raj; but here the dominating influence was that of the Mughals. The raja had no power. His minister had entire authority. The position of the Peshwa was rather anomalous. He was nominally the chief officer of the independent Hindu king of Satara; but he held several subahs nominally under the Emperor of Delhi. With the exception of the Raja of Mysore and the Raja of Satara, all the rulers were nominally subordinate to the Emperor of Delhi, though the emperor himself was an exiled wanderer.

BOOK III.—THE EUROPEANS IN INDIA

CHAPTER I

EARLY SETTLEMENTS

Order of European Settlements.—From a period of remote antiquity all the races that entered India came by land. This was true till the end of the fifteenth century, when the people of Western Europe began to arrive in the country. They came by sea. Their first object was trade, and only as a result of their efforts to extend their trade or their religion did conquest follow. The Portuguese, who were known in India by the term Firingi, came first. After them came the people of Holland, known as the Olandaz. Then came the English, and last of all the French, who are known as the Farasis.

Early Trade between India and Europe.—From the time of Alexander the Great, the people of Eastern Europe had carried on a trade with India. During the ascendency of the Khalifas the Arabs managed to get possession of the trade of India and of that of the Indian Archipelago. They used to sell Indian products, such as silk and cotton piece-goods, and spices, to the merchants of Venice and Genoa. These carried the products to Western and Northern Europe, where they sold them at an immense profit. The trade with India was for centuries almost a monopoly of these two republics. The English, French, Portuguese, and other nations were anxious to do away with this monopoly; but the only way to India hitherto known lay through the Mediterranean and the Red Sea, and Venice and Genoa were masters of the Mediterranean, and the Arabs were supreme in the Red Sea. To increase still further the difficulties of communication between East and West, the Turks, who made themselves masters of Western Asia and of Egypt, discouraged and greatly hampered the transit trade.

New Routes.—Thus the only resource left to the people of Western Europe was the discovery of a new route. Some explorers thought that they would reach India by crossing the sea westwards. The expeditions that were sent out in search of the western route, however, did not discover India, but a far larger continent. The discoverer, Columbus, believed the new land found by him to be India, and so it was named New India, or the West Indies, and the copper-coloured aborigines were named the West Indians. Other navigators thought that they would reach India by following a north-western route, and many expeditions were fitted out for the discovery of such a passage. These expeditions were unsuccessful. Only within the last century has a passage round the north coast of the American continent been proved possible. But the efforts to find a north-west passage were not without result; they, at any rate, greatly added to our knowledge of the geography of the Arctic seas. Some explorers, again, thought to reach India by doubling the southern extremity of Africa. These at last succeeded. Vasco da Gama, a celebrated navigator of Portugal, doubled the Cape of Good Hope in 1498, and succeeded in reaching India. He landed at Calicut, then ruled by a petty chief with the title of Zamorin, and the Portuguese trade began to flourish.

The Portuguese and the Dutch.—The Portuguese occupied Goa, a place belonging to the kingdom of Bijapur. They made it the capital of their possessions in the Indian seas, and directed their attention to the extension of their commercial and political influence in the Eastern Peninsula and in the eastern islands. In Bengal they settled at Hughli, and for a time were masters of Chittagong and Arakan. Independent bands of Portuguese became pirates, and harassed the Subahdar of Bengal for several generations. The most important of their possessions was Ceylon, from which they were expelled by the Dutch, who by the end of the sixteenth century became masters of the Indian seas, conquered and colonized the island of Java, and settled at Chinsurah in Bengal, and Porto Novo in Southern India. The Dutch were in their turn succeeded by the English.

The English East India Company.—The East India Company received a charter from Queen Elizabeth in 1599. In the course of a century the Company established factories for trade at Calcutta, Madras, and Bombay. At Madras and at Bombay the sites of the cities belonged to it in full sovereignty; but at Calcutta the Company was a subject of the Great Mughal, though it had all the rights of a Zemindar.

The French East India Company and Dupleix.—The French East India Company received its charter in 1664, and sent squadrons to the Indian seas. In Southern India the French settled at Pondicherry, and in Bengal at Faras-danga. Dupleix was the greatest Frenchman ever sent to India. He was for several years Governor of Chandarnagar, or Farasdanga, and raised it from the position of an Indian village to that of a great city and centre of trade. He was then transferred to Pondicherry, where he determined, by fomenting quarrels among the native states, and interfering in their affairs, to establish a French empire in India. He interfered in the affairs of the independent subahdars of the Karnatik and the Deccan, and in the course of a few years his nominees were ruling at Hyderabad and at Arcot, and he was, next to the Peshwa, the most important man south of the Vindhyas.

Robert Clive captures Arcot.—The English were the great rivals of Dupleix; but for many years they were not in a position to cope with him. At last a greater genius even than the great Frenchman appeared among the English in the person of Clive, a writer in the Madras establishment of the East India Company. Following the example of Dupleix the English took the part of the unsuccessful candidate for the subahdarship of the Karnatik. Their candidate was, however, at first unsuccessful, and was reduced to great straits. He took refuge in the fort of Trichinopoly, which was besieged by the combined Muhammadan and French army. Everything seemed lost. Everywhere in Southern India the French were triumphant. Then Clive formed the plan of attacking Arcot, the capital of the Karnatik, and so causing a diver-

Lord Clive

sion in favour of Muhammad Ali, the candidate supported by the English. His plan succeeded. He captured Arcot, but was in his turn besieged by the enemy. With remarkable bravery and power of endurance he not only defended the fort, but compelled the enemy to raise the siege. This achievement not only raised Clive, who was termed "a heaven-born general" by the Prime Minister of England, to sudden fame; but it added greatly to the reputation of the English in India. The defence of Arcot was the turning-point in the struggle.

Dupleix and Clive.—Dupleix and Clive were both men of genius; but Clive was supported by the English government of the day, while Dupleix, notwithstanding his great services to his country, was superseded and recalled. Almost immediately after the defence of Arcot, Clive was forced to return to England on account of his health; but his success had saved the English position in India. Dupleix remained some years longer in power, and the war in India continued to be carried on; but the British position was never again desperate.

Destruction of French Power.—In the course of a few years after the recall of Dupleix, the dream of a French empire vanished into thin air, and even their capital in India was in the hands of the British. The British generously restored it to them, and they have never since seriously troubled the British as rivals. The victory of Wandewash, the surrender of Pondicherry, and the capture of the hill fortress of Gingi, left the British the virtual masters of the Karnatik.

CHAPTER II

THE COMPANY OBTAINS IMMENSE TERRITORY

Quarrel with Siraj.—The veteran Subahdar of Bengal, Ali Vardi Khan, was succeeded by a young and weak-headed prince, Sirajuddaula, his daughter's son. Siraj was not well-disposed towards the British. On the pretext that they were sheltering his enemies, Siraj attacked the British settlement at Calcutta, took the fort by storm, plundered the treasury, occupied the town, and expelled the British. His general, Manik Chand, murdered cruelly 123 of the British, by confining the captives to the number of 146 in a small room called the Black Hole. This room was the garrison prison, where soldiers guilty of misdemeanours were temporarily confined. It was some eighteen feet square, and whether intentional or unintentional, no more fiendish form of cruelty could have been devised than to confine such a number of prisoners in such a place. It was the news of this massacre that induced the Madras Government to send Clive to Bengal. Clive was back again from England, his health restored, and had been made governor of Fort St. David.

Clive Recaptures Calcutta.—He found no difficulty in re-occupying Calcutta; and then, in order to punish the Nawab, he captured the port of Hughli, then regarded as the royal port of Bengal. He attacked the camp of the Nawab, who had a second time advanced to Calcutta; and, though not as successful as he had hoped, he forced the Nawab to make an offensive and defensive alliance. The French being at war with Britain, Clive captured Chandarnagar and kept possession of it. Some of the principal officers of the Nawab, aided by some of the leading zamindars, were now plotting to set aside Sirajuddaula, as his rule had, for various reasons, become hateful to them. Doubtful of their power to cope successfully with a subahdar who had so many resources, they tried to draw the British into the plot against that ruler.

Victory at Plassey, 1757.—They found Clive ready to listen to them. On the pretext of settling some difficulties with the Nawab, he proceeded with a small but well-disciplined army towards Murshidabad. The Nawab advanced to meet him at the head of a force twenty times more numerous. The armies met at Plassey. Sirajuddaula was defeated and fled. Followed to the capital he again took to flight; but he was captured, brought back, and put to death by Mir Jaffar.

Victory at Baxar, 1764.—The successful party now placed Mir Jaffar on the throne, but the British became the real masters of the provinces of Bengal and Behar. Though for a short time Mir Kasim, the son-in-law and successor of Mir Jaffar, resisted British authority, his defeat in 1764 in two pitched battles put an end to the war in these provinces. Driven from Bengal, Kasim formed an alliance with the nominal Emperor of Hindustan and with the Nawab Vizier of Oudh, whose sway extended from the Karamnasa to Cawnpur, and invaded Behar. Sir Thomas Munro, a veteran British soldier, decisively defeated the allies at the battle of Baxar. Clive was not then in Bengal. He came back after the battle.

The Emperor grants Divani of Bengal to the Company.—The British were now the real masters of Bengal; but they had no legal position. They were simply the servants of the Nawab. Clive therefore applied for and obtained from the emperor the *divani* or right to collect the revenues of these provinces. The emperor, in lieu of this grant, obtained an annual tribute of 26 *lakhs* of rupees, and the provinces of Kora and Allahabad. After the battle of Baxar the English could have made themselves masters of the whole of Hindustan, but they generously restored Oudh and Benares to the Nawab of Oudh.

Oudh a Protectorate.—From that time the Nawab was the friend of the British and relied upon them for the protection of his territories. To secure this end, the English conquered Rohilkhand for the Nawab in 1774. This gave him a well-defined frontier in the west, viz. the river Ganges, which the Marhatta horsemen could not ford, and the British were relieved of their anxieties of a possible union of the Rohillas with the Marhattas to the detriment of British power.

The Double System of Government and the Famine.—On receipt of the *divani*, a sort of Double Government was established in Bengal. The collection of revenue, the civil courts, and the military government remained in the hands of the British, while the punishment of criminals was carried on by the Nawab. This double system was very troublesome to the people. They did not know whom to obey. They had too many masters. The consequence was disorganization. This was followed by a terrible famine, which destroyed nearly a third of the population.

Appointment of a Governor-General.—The British government saw that in the course of a few years a body of merchants trading with India, the English East India Company, had become the rulers of vast provinces and masters of immense revenues. They also saw the necessity of controlling the Company in its management of the British possessions in India. Therefore, in 1773, they passed an act of parliament appointing the Governor of Bengal to be the Governor-general of all British India. They gave him a council of four members to assist him with their advice, and they established a Supreme Court of Justice in Calcutta. The Governor-general was to be the servant of the East India Company. This act is called the Regulating Act.

CHAPTER III

BRITAIN A GREAT POWER IN INDIA

Warren Hastings was the first Governor-general. Three of his councillors came from Britain. They knew nothing of India, but they formed the majority in the Council. Hastings was in the minority, and in the management of affairs was greatly harassed by the opposition of the majority of the Council. So powerless did he feel himself that once he thought of resigning. But the death of one of the councillors put Hastings in power, and he ruled India with wisdom up to the year 1785.

Wars in Bombay, &c.—During this time the Company had to engage in numerous wars in Bombay and in Madras. The cost of these wars was considerable, and the demands of the Company at home for money were pressing. Hastings was therefore often in need of money. He adopted various means for raising it, and his enemies both in India and in England blamed him for the means he had adopted.

His Trial.—He, however, steered the vessel of the state clear of all danger, and consolidated the Empire that had been established by the generalship of Clive. On his return to England he was tried in Parliament for some of his acts while

Warren Hastings

Governor-general, but after a seven years' trial he was honourably acquitted.

Hastings was engaged in two great wars, one with Mysore, and the other with the Marhattas in Bombay.

CHAPTER IV

THE MYSORE WARS

Haidar Ali.—Mysore was at one time a Hindu principality ruled by the Yadavas. On the destruction of the kingdom of Vijayanagar it became independent. During the course of a century and a half the kingdom extended its boundaries on all sides. About 1733 its affairs fell into disorder. The royal family was weak, and the chief power in the state was in the hands of the minister, Nandi Raj. He had a Muhammadan adventurer in his employ who gradually rose to a high position. This man was Haidar Ali, who, in 1761, imprisoned the royal family, set the minister aside, and assumed supreme power in the state, with the title Sultan. He rapidly conquered all the country to the banks of the Krishna. He had very great troubles, however, with the Marhattas and the Nizam. He bought off the Marhattas by a money payment; but the cunning Nizam (the title by which the Subahdar of the Deccan has come to be known) involved him in a war with the British.

First War.—In the first war Haidar gained much. While the main armies were engaged at a distance, Haidar with a strong detachment suddenly presented himself before the gates of Madras, and the Council in panic entered into an offensive and defensive alliance with him. This was in 1769. The terms of the treaty were not observed by either side, and so there was mutual dissatisfaction.

Second War and Haidar's Death.—About 1778 Britain, being at war with France, wanted to occupy the French settlement of Mahé, which was in Haidar's dominions. Haidar protested. The Madras Council paid no heed to his protests, and so the second Mysore War ensued. Haidar was always ready. He made the Karnatik the theatre of war, and was often assisted by the Dutch and the French navies. The British at Madras were hard pushed. Hastings sent armies from Bengal, which passed through Orissa and the Northern Circars to the relief of the Madras Presidency. The war was hotly contested. After his first successes he suffered several reverses. But notwithstanding this the British were greatly relieved by the news of Haidar's death.

Tipu Succeeds.—Haidar was succeeded by Tipu, who, though not equal to his father in ability, was equally hostile to Britain. The war dragged on its slow length for some time, and was terminated by the Treaty of Mangalore, according to which each party remained in the same position in which it was before the war.

Tipu Sultan

Tipu Defeated. Ceded Territory. —Tipu ruled with an iron hand. His territories had never before been under any Muhammadan government. Orthodox Hindus were the principal inhabitants. Tipu forcibly converted many thousands of them to Muhammadanism. Many old Brahmans committed suicide to escape conversion. The Marhattas protested and invaded his kingdom, but were bought off by a cession of territory. Tipu invaded Travancore, which was under British protection, and so the British declared war against him. Lord Cornwallis asked the Marhattas and the Nizam to join him. The combined armies invaded Mysore, took fort after fort, defeated Tipu in two general engagements, and were preparing to lay siege to Seringapatam, his capital, when Tipu, thoroughly frightened, made peace with them by ceding half his territories to the allies. The conquests thus made were equally divided by the allies. Lord Cornwallis compelled Tipu to send two of his sons as hostages to Calcutta.

He Intrigues with the French.—The next Governor-general, Sir John Shore, allowed the sons to join their father, and Tipu was found intriguing with the French, and with the native states, with the intention of expelling the British from India. The French were at this time very powerful in Europe. Napoleon with a strong army was in Egypt. The position was full of danger.

Defeat and Death of Tipu.—Lord Wellesley, therefore, immediately on his arrival in India as Governor-general, thought it necessary to put down the intrigues of the restless Tipu. He declared war against him, carried it on with vigour, took Seringapatam by storm, put an end to the Muhammadan kingdom of Mysore and restored the Yadava Raja to his ancient possessions. The rest of the territory of Tipu he annexed to the British Empire. He also pensioned off the Nawab of the Karnatik and the Raja of Tanjore, the descendant of Shaji. Thus was formed the Madras Presidency, which, from the death of Tipu in 1799 up to the present day, has never been disturbed by war or commotion.

CHAPTER V

THE MARHATTA WARS

The Struggle for the Marhatta Peshwaship.—After the battle of Panipat in 1761, Balaji Baji Rao died, and was succeeded by his son, Madhu Rao, a minor, and his brother, Raghava, was appointed regent. Raghava was an able man and a good general, but extremely unscrupulous. On attaining his majority Madhu Rao tried his best to live on good terms with his uncle, but was compelled to put him under restraint shortly after. Madhu Rao, though young, was a good ruler and a good soldier. He was successful in war and in administration. He always selected good men to serve him. But he did not live long. He died in 1774. His uncle killed his brother and successor, Narayan Rao, and tried to make himself Peshwa; but he was opposed by the ministers of the state, who raised Madhava Rao, the infant son of Madhu Rao, to the Peshwaship, and compelled Raghava to fly for protection to the British at Bombay. The British espoused his cause, and sent armies into the Marhatta country both from Bombay and from Calcutta. Raghava denied that Madhu, who was a posthumous child, was his nephew's son, and claimed the office of Peshwa. The war proceeded slowly.

Madhu Rao

Nana Farnavis.—Nana Farnavis was the ruling spirit at Poona. He never engaged in pitched battles with the British, but always harassed them in the Marhatta style of warfare, plundering their convoys, and laying waste territory belonging to them or their allies. Nana had a great supporter in Mahadevji Sindhia, the son of Ranaji Sindhia. The war was brought to a close by the Treaty of Salbai in 1782. By this treaty the British obtained Salsette. Raghava secured a considerable pension, but had to give up the sovereignty to the child Madhu.

Mutual Jealousies of Marhatta Confederates.—The interval between the Treaty of Salbai and the Second Marhatta War in 1803 was disturbed by the mutual jealousies of Holkar and Sindhia, Nana and Sindhia, Nana and Baji Rao II, son of Raghava, who succeeded to the Peshwaship in 1795. The chief events during this period were the conquest of the Subahs of Delhi and Agra by Sindhia, and the victory of Kurdla, obtained in 1795 by the combined Marhatta forces against the Nizam. This victory threw that potentate into the arms of the British, who thenceforward treated him in the same way as they did the Nawab-vizier of Oudh, *i.e.* as an ally under protection.

Holkar and Baji Rao II.—As long, however, as Nana Farnavis lived there was something like a combination among the Marhatta chiefs; but shortly after his death, in 1800, Holkar led a large army to Poona. Baji Rao greatly dreaded Holkar, whose brother had been captured by him, and cruelly put to death. He, therefore, fled for protection to the British, in Bombay, signed the treaty of Bassein, by which he consented to remain under British protection on the same conditions as the Nizam and the Nawab-vizier. The British re-established him at Poona. Sindhia, Holkar, and the Raja of Nagpur were enraged at the nominal head of the Marhatta confederacy placing himself under British protection. They were all rulers of extensive dominions, had large armies disciplined by French generals, and possessed in addition immense resources. They thought they were placed in a very false position. They were subordinate to the Peshwa. The Peshwa was under British protection. The natural inference, they thought, was that they were also under British protection. This they could not tolerate; so they combined to make war upon the Peshwa's protectors.

Marhatta War with British, 1802–1805.—Holkar was never very friendly to Sindhia, whose efforts to destroy him and his family had several times seemed on the point of proving successful. He therefore held aloof for a whole year, during which Sindhia and the Raja of Nagpur were attacked from the north, south, and west. They were in fact hemmed in. They fought well, but the British arms prevailed. Sir Arthur Wellesley, afterwards Lord Wellington, and brother of Lord Wellesley, the Governor-general, defeated the Marhatta army at Assaye and at Argaon, while Lord Lake defeated them at Laswari. Both rulers were obliged to purchase peace by ceding a considerable portion of their territories. The British obtained Orissa, Agra, and Delhi by this war.

War with Holkar.—Holkar then took the field, invaded Northern India, plundered Mathura and Farukkabad, and harassed the British army for a year, but was compelled at last to sue for peace.

Intrigues of Baji Rao II against British.—But by this time a change had come over the spirit of British administration. The Governor-general received orders from Britain not to interfere with the affairs of native states unless their rulers actually invaded British territory, and so the Marhattas continued to disturb the peace of Central India for a period of twelve years more. During all these years Baji Rao was constantly intriguing with the Marhatta and other Indian powers against the British. He began to save money, the sinews of war. He confiscated the states of the Marhatta *jagirdars* who were opposed to the interests of his father and himself. He became so troublesome that the British were compelled, in 1817, to make a fresh treaty with him, curtailing his power of treating with other native states of India without the permission of his British protectors. This was, in fact, abolishing his headship of the Marhatta confederacy, and made Baji Rao extremely discontented; so he sought an opportunity for revenge.

War with Pindaris and Marhattas, 1816.—The Pindaris were plundering bands of horsemen who followed the Marhatta armies, and in the early years of their existence served as irregular auxiliaries, but on the organization of regular armies by the Marhatta chiefs they were dismissed and compelled to shift for themselves. The only Marhatta kingdom in which they found favour was that of Holkar, who still maintained a large body of Pindari irregulars. These robber bands devastated the whole of Central India, and at last attacked British territory, and so the British had to take steps to put them down. The Pindaris were easily dispersed, and Holkar's army was defeated with great slaughter at Mahidpur. But the intrigues of Baji Rao bore fruit. The Raja of Nagpur and Baji Rao himself attacked the Residencies in their respective capitals, and thus hostilities commenced. There was very little fighting. The British easily conquered and annexed the Peshwa's territories, and took the infant Raja of Nagpur under their protection. Thus ended the Third Mahratta War, and the Bombay Presidency was formed. The Raja of Satara was restored to his ancient Raj.

Marhatta Power finally Suppressed, 1843.—Only once more had the British had trouble with the Marhattas. During the minority of Jayaji Rao Sindhia there were two parties in the kingdom, one friendly and the other unfriendly to Britain. For a short time the latter gained the ascendency and secured the support of the army. This induced the Governor-general, in 1843, to send an army into the Gwalior territory to remove the unfriendly nobles from power and to reduce the army. Since then the relations of the government with Sindhia have continued to be very friendly. For certain reasons the British had to keep possession of the fort of Gwalior. In 1885 this was restored to the Maharaja, and the attachment of the Sindhia family to the British Government is now very sincere.

CHAPTER VI

THE NEPAL AND THE BURMESE WARS

Gurkha Conquest of Nepal and War with British, 1814.—When Lord Clive and Warren Hastings were struggling to secure for the East India Company what was virtually the sovereignty in Bengal, a sturdy race of Hill Rajputs, from one of the numerous valleys into which the Sub-Himalayan regions are divided, invaded Nepal under their distinguished leader,

Prithvi Narayan. They conquered the three or four small independent principalities into which that small valley was divided, and in the course of a quarter of a century made themselves masters of all the mountain regions from Sikim to Kangra. They had their troubles with China, but they managed to appease her by a nominal submission in 1792. Later they advanced some obsolete claims to two small districts in British India, and these they occupied. This led to a war with India. After three years of hard fighting, in which many lives were lost, the British succeeded in obtaining large cessions of mountainous territories, and in appointing a Resident at Khatmandu. The hill-sanatorias in the North-Western Provinces have all been established in the mountain districts ceded by Nepal.

First Burmese War, 1825 – 1826.—By the end of the eighteenth and the beginning of the nineteenth century the Burmese had made themselves masters of nearly the whole of the eastern coast of the Bay of Bengal and much of the inland territory. They conquered Assam, and thus became a neighbouring and hostile power. After a short time they occupied an island in the Bay of Bengal belonging to Britain. The King of Burma was so audacious as to send a golden chain to tie down the Governor-general and bring him to Ava. This first Burmese war, 1825–26, was one of the most expensive the British Government ever undertook in the East. They had to contend not so much with a powerful and a warlike enemy, as with malaria, inundation, dearth of food, and so on. Sir A. Campbell, however, succeeded in bringing the war to a glorious conclusion. The British occupied Assam, Arakan, and the Tenasserim Provinces, and obtained a large war indemnity.

Second Burmese War, 1852.—The Burmese were the most perverse and unreasonable people with whom the British Government had yet had to deal. After the first war they might have shown themselves friendly to the British Government, a neighbour at once kind-hearted, considerate, civilized, and powerful; but the Burmese were sullen. The British agent at Ava did not receive due respect, and at last the Government discontinued sending an agent. In 1852 various governors were appointed in succession at Rangoon, who distinguished themselves by manifesting their hatred of the British. One went so far as to fire at a British ship from the ramparts of the fort. This led to the Second Burmese War. The people of Lower Burma were so much oppressed that they hailed the invaders with delight. Fort after fort and city after city were occupied by British troops, and the war at last came to an end because there was no enemy to fight. At the close of the war Rangoon, Prome, and other districts were annexed to the British dominions.

Third Burmese War, 1885.—The Burmese government still continued hostile. British merchants were unfairly treated, and could obtain no redress for their grievances. The French and the Italians intrigued at the court of Ava. Dacoity and confusion were the order of the day. The Government of India again reminded the Burmese of their duty, again and again demanded that they should consider the just interests of the British merchants, but all in vain. A third war was declared in 1885. There was no battle. Steamers from Rangoon proceeded up the Irawady; a small army was landed at Mandalay; King Theebaw was captured and brought to Ratnagiri, where he is still living as a state pensioner and prisoner. In 1886 Burma was annexed to the British Empire. The most touching incident of the war was the devotion displayed by the Queen Supialat towards her husband, the banished king. She volunteered to accompany him and share his fate.

CHAPTER VII

THE SIKH WARS

Persecution of Sikhs by Muhammadans.—Three hundred years of close contact with a foreign power and a foreign religion produced in the fifteenth and sixteenth centuries a large number of reformers among the Hindus. One of these was Guru Nanak, a native of the Punjab, who preached a new form of faith. For several generations his followers were quiet and peaceful. But the Muhammadans hated and persecuted them. The cruelties practised by the Muhammadans at last produced a spirit of retaliation, and the Sikhs formed themselves into something like an army. The Emperor Bahadur Shah tried to put down their military power, but in vain.

Ahmad Shah tries to Subdue them.—After the signal victory gained by him at Panipat, Ahmad Shah Abdali returned to Afghanistan, and the Sikhs issued from their mountain fastnesses and took possession of the whole of the Punjab. They constructed numerous forts to secure their new possession, and practised great barbarities on the Musalmans. This induced Ahmad Shah Abdali to send his commander-in-chief to the Punjab in 1762. But the Sikhs put him to flight, drove away the Subahdar appointed by the Abdali kings at Lahore, and took possession of the city. Ahmad Shah twice returned to the Punjab to punish them; but, as soon as he appeared on the scene, the Sikhs retired to their forts, and when he withdrew they again took possession of the country.

Their Form of Government.—They formed themselves into eleven *misls* or bands, some tribal and some territorial; and these had their head-quarters in different parts of the country. During the reign of Aurangzeb, two of the younger sons of Guru Govinda had been buried alive at Sirhind. The Sikhs in 1763 invested the city in great force, killed all its Musalman inhabitants, and razed it to the ground. When Ahmad Shah came to the Punjab for the last time in 1768, the misls were the real masters of the country. In 1792 Ranajit Singh succeeded to the small principality established by his grandfather, Chhatter Singh.

Ranajit Singh's Conquests.—On succeeding his father in the leadership of the Sukarchakia Misl, the first endeavour of Ranajit was to bring under his control the misls to the west of the Sutlej. He saved the country from an invasion by the Afghans. He conquered Lahore from the three Sikh chiefs who had held different parts of it from the time of the expulsion of Abdali's subahdar, and established his capital there. In 1801 he assumed the title of Maharaja, and began to coin money in his own name. The Musalmans rose against him several times, but he put them down with a strong hand. In quick succession he conquered Kashmir, Jamu, Multan, Bannu, Dera Ghazi Khan, Dera Ismail Khan, and other places.

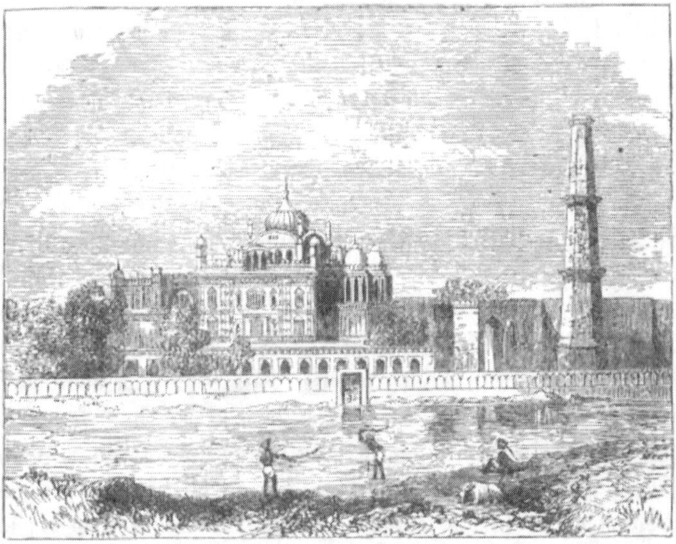

Ranajit Singh's Tomb

Then he turned his attention to the Sikh Misls to the east of the Sutlej, but in 1809 they placed themselves under the protection of the British. Ranajit's kingdom has been destroyed, but the Sikh principalities to the east of the Sutlej are still in existence, the last remains of the past glory of the great Sikh nation.

Sikhs' Restlessness.—Ranajit died in 1839. The Sikhs were a lawless, restless people. It was only the strong hand of Ranajit that kept them quiet. As soon as that hand was removed they displayed their national characteristics. His eldest son and his grandson died in the course of two or three years, not without suspicion being roused of their having been treacherously done to death. His second son was assassinated. His third, a young child of seven years, was raised to the throne. The Sikh *Sardars* were busy killing one another.

First Sikh War.—At last the army got the upper hand. The Maharani, in order to get rid of it, induced the soldiers to invade British territory. The British were unprepared, and the Sikh army marched several miles beyond their frontier. Four pitched battles were fought. The Sikhs, who had been carefully drilled in the European fashion, displayed great bravery, but the British gained the victory. The Doab between the Sutlej and the Ravi was annexed to the British Empire. Kashmir was sold to Golab Singh to enable the Lahore *Darbar* to pay the war indemnity demanded by the Indian Government. A Resident was stationed at Lahore, and he became the President of the Council of Regency.

Second Sikh War.—Within three years the Sikhs again displayed a turbulent spirit. Two British officers were murdered at Multan. The Sikh *Sardars* in the north and west rose in rebellion. A battle was fought at Chillianwalla in which the Sikhs gained some advantage, but they were utterly routed at Guzerat in 1849.

The whole of the Punjab was then annexed to the British dominions. The Kohinur, which belonged to Ranajit, was sent as a present to Queen Victoria, and Maharaja Dhulip Singh was granted a pension of five lakhs of rupees. He became a Christian, and settled in England, where he died.

CHAPTER VIII

GENEROSITY OF BRITISH POLICY

Kerauli and Satara.—The Rajas of Kerauli and Satara died soon after the second Sikh war. Both had adopted children. Lord Dalhousie held that the State of Satara was created by the English, and, therefore, on the failure of the direct line, they were not bound to give it to an adopted child. Kerauli was an ancient state, not created by the English, and accordingly he held that the succession there should be determined by ancient custom. The Court of Directors and the Board of Control agreeing with his lordship, Satara was annexed to British India.

Nana Saheb, Jhansi and Nagpur.—Baji Rao, the ex-Peshwa, died in 1853, and his pension lapsed to the state. His adopted son, Nana Saheb, made several efforts to get the pension granted to him, but in vain. It was proposed to remove the descendants of Bahadur Shah from the imperial palace at Delhi; and the Rajas of Jhansi and Nagpur dying without issue, these states were annexed.

Lord W. C. Bentinck

Treatment of Nawab of Oudh.—The Nawabs of Oudh had been for a long time the protégés of the British, who had raised them to the dignity of kings. But their administration of the country had been always unsatisfactory. Lord Hardinge had consequently written to the king, warning him that if it did not improve in two years it would be taken out of his hands. But even this did not bring the king to his senses, and in 1856 the Directors ordered the annexation of the country. Lord Dalhousie, though he did not approve of the measure, loyally carried out the orders of his superiors, and the state was annexed. Wajid Ali Shah was brought to

Calcutta, and a pension of Rs. 1,200,000 was settled on him.

Early Aims of British.—A rapid sketch has been given above of the formation of the British Indian Empire. The British have come into possession of this vast empire in spite of themselves. They were traders, and were anxious to secure opportunities for trading. Their physicians cured Mughal princesses, and took no reward except privileges for their national trade. This speaks volumes for their patriotism and their spirit of self-sacrifice for the public good. They engaged in war with native states simply because these states refused them the same privileges as they granted their rivals. The idea of founding an empire was not theirs. It was formulated by the Frenchman Dupleix. They got the better of the French, managed to humiliate them; and as the French were their national enemies, they were delighted. They were delighted also that the Subahdars of Bengal and the Karnatik were their friends, and were grateful to them for important services rendered to their trade. For years they left the subahdars to manage their own affairs, but the whole machinery of government in India was out of order, and so they were forced to interfere on several occasions.

Their Hesitation to Assume Rule.—Still they hesitated to meddle with the government of the country. In Bengal they first took the Dewani, *i.e.* obtained a legal footing, not as rulers, but as befitted a company of merchants, as financiers. After the battle of Baxar they restored the whole country from Karamnasa to Cawnpur to the Emperor and the Nawab of Oudh. In the Mysore wars they divided the ceded territories with the Nizam and the Marhattas, though in their conquest these played but a very subordinate part.

Their Treatment of Conquered Rulers.—They were always kind and considerate to potentates who lost their dominions in wars with them. The large and influential Mysore family, and the still more influential Oudh family in the neighbourhood of Calcutta, are examples of British consideration for fallen greatness. All over the country there are political pensioners whom the Government of India supports most generously. To the native princes they are always kindly and courteous.

Their Treatment of Native Sovereigns.—They treat them as sovereigns, bound only by the articles of the treaties with them. The principal conditions of these treaties are that the British grant them military protection in consideration either of an annual money payment or a cession of territory, and that the states have no power to employ Europeans in their service, and have no political relations beyond their own territories. These are the principal conditions of what is known as the Subsidiary Alliances, by which most of the native princes are bound to the paramount power. Nothing can be more liberal than these terms. The native princes, relieved of all fears of interference from without, can freely develop the resources of their country, and be as rich and prosperous as their ability will allow.

Their Generosity to their Subjects.—Nor are the British less generous in dealing with their own subjects. The permanent settlement in Bengal and in Benares, the cause of the exceptional prosperity of these two great provinces, is a notable instance of the spirit of self-sacrifice of the British Indian Government for the good of their subjects. The permanent settlement transferred the Government's rights in land to a body of Zemindars, who thus became land-owners whose interests it was to increase the productiveness of the country.

Their Humanity.—The British have abolished many cruel rites once prevalent in India. Who will not shudder at the commencement of the twentieth century at the idea of throwing the first-born children into the estuary of the Ganges? Who will not shudder at the idea of parents killing infant girls because they are not in a position to bestow them in marriage in suitable families? Who will not shudder at the idea of burning widows at the funeral pyre of their husbands? Yet a hundred years ago these cruel and inhuman acts were of everyday occurrence, and it is the humanity of the British rulers that has saved India from these abominations.

BOOK IV.—BRITISH EMPIRE

CHAPTER I

THE SEPOY MUTINY

British Army in India.—The British army in India always consisted of some regiments of British and some of native soldiers. The native regiments were disciplined in the European fashion and officered by Europeans. The succession of brilliant victories gained by the British Government during the first half of the nineteenth century, in all of which the Sepoys had done good service, made the latter believe that they had won the victories and that they were the masters of the situation. Lord Napier, when Commander-in-Chief, foretold that the Sepoys would mutiny one day, and wished to take stringent preventive measures. He quarrelled with Lord Dalhousie on the subject of the military reform necessary for the prevention of such a mutiny, and the Government not agreeing with him he had to resign.

Causes of Native Unrest in 1856.—For the whole of the year 1856 the Indian mind was greatly agitated. Since coming to India as Governor-general, Lord Dalhousie had annexed several of the native states, and the claimants to the sovereignties of these had numerous sympathizers all over India. The old state of things seemed to have passed away. Measures of reform were introduced; marriage of widows was legalized; a great impetus was given to English education; the education of females was taken in hand; great railway projects were started; telegraph lines were laid. People thought that the British wanted to make India another Britain. Designing men spread all sorts of wild rumours. It was asserted that the British were going to convert the whole nation to Christianity. At this time Enfield rifles were given to the native soldiers. The cartridges used for this gun had to be bitten by the teeth, and a rumour was spread abroad that these cartridges were greased with the fat of hogs and oxen in order to defile the Muhammadans and Hindus alike.

The Mutiny.—Signs of mutiny were first shown at Barrackpur, but they were soon suppressed. At Meerut the Sepoys rose in mutiny, broke open the jails, killed the European officers, and marched to Delhi, where they saluted the old imbecile Bahadur Shah, the then eldest member of the old imperial family, as their Badshah. Mutineers from other stations came up to Delhi. The mutineers of Cawnpur were on their way to Delhi when Nana Saheb, the adopted son of Baji Rao II, induced them to return, to massacre the Europeans at Cawnpur, and to prepare for a struggle with the British. At Lucknow the adherents of the deposed king rose in rebellion, and were joined by many of the old Talukdars. At Jhansi the Rani took the lead and killed seventy Europeans in the station.

Lord Dalhousie

The Measures for its Suppression.—The British sent three armies against the mutineers; one from the Punjab, one from Bengal, and a third from Bombay. The Punjab army, under General Wilson, besieged and captured Delhi; the Bengal army, under Havelock and Neil, relieved the garrison at Lucknow; and the Bombay army, under Sir Hugh Rose, relieved Jhansi. But at the last moment, when the Mutiny in Northern India was almost at an end, all India was startled at the fall of Gwalior into the hands of the mutinous soldiery of the Sindhia, led by Tantia Topi. After some fighting this rising also was suppressed. But bands of mutinous soldiers and numbers of rebels from among the people, headed by Nana Saheb and others, were still roving about the country. Sir Colin Campbell, the Commander-in-Chief, reorganized the horse-artillery, and by means of it he dispersed these people wherever they collected. The last operation of the Mutiny was the capture of Lucknow. As soon as military operations ceased, Earl Canning granted a general pardon to all who had been engaged in the Mutiny, with the exception of those who had taken part in the killing of Europeans. The measures adopted by Canning inspired confidence all over the empire, and its loyalty has never since been shaken.

General Havelock

Company's Power Abolished.—The Mutiny and the loss of British life at the hands of the Sepoys created a deep impression in Britain, and it was thought desirable that the East India Company should be abolished, and the administration placed directly under the control of the Queen and Parliament. Accordingly, the Company was abolished, and the Company's Governor-general was made the Viceroy of the Queen, and a proclamation was issued by which all grounds of suspicion of tampering with caste or religious faith were removed.

Progress since India came under the Crown.—About fifty years have elapsed since the assumption of the direct administration of affairs by Her Majesty the late Queen Victoria. These years have been years of steady progress. There has been no great disturbance of peace. There have been wars indeed, but they have been beyond the borders of India. But within India, peace has reigned throughout the length and breadth of the land.

CHAPTER II

RULE OF THE VICEROYS

Lord Elgin (1862–1863). Sir John Lawrence (1864–1869).—Lord Elgin succeeded Lord Canning, but he died soon after his arrival in India, at Dharmsala, in the Punjab. On his death, Sir William Denison acted for a short time as Viceroy of India. Ultimately Sir John Lawrence, who had been the Chief Commissioner of the Punjab during the Mutiny, was appointed Governor-general. One of the objects of his appointment was the suppression of the rising of the Musalmans of Sitana on the Punjab frontier; and the first act of his administration was the despatch of Sir Hugh Rose, the Commander-in-Chief, to that place. The rising was put down, but at a great cost of men and money.

Sir John Lawrence

War with Bhutan.—The British made their first treaty with the Devaraj of Bhutan in the year 1772. Since then there have been many political revolutions in that country. The Dharmaraj was, in theory, the supreme ruler, both in religious and in temporal affairs. He used to appoint a Divan for the management of temporal affairs, and this Divan was the Devaraj. When a Dharmaraj or a Devaraj died search was made throughout the country for a boy with certain marks on his body, who, when found, was appointed to the vacant situation. About the year 1860, two provincial governors were very powerful. They were the Tanso Penlo and Pero Penlo. The former was hostile to the British, and often led raiding expeditions into Assam and Bengal. He appointed his own Dharmaraj and Devaraj, and occupied the Doars in Assam. These were the passes by which hillmen descended into the plains, and they had come into the possession of the British on the conquest of Assam. The Bengal Doars, too, had subsequently fallen into their hands, and they paid an annual subsidy for all these Doars to the Bhutanese. On Tanso Penlo's assuming an attitude of open hostility, the Government of Bengal sent Sir Ashley Eden as ambassador to the Devaraj, with whom the Government were in treaty. But the insolent conduct of Tanso Penlo defeated the object of the embassy, and there was no alternative left but war. Two forts, Divangiri and Dalimkot, fell into the hands of the British, but the country being very unhealthy, they concluded a peace by which a formal cession was made of all the conquered passes and the neighbouring land, and the subsidy to Bhutan was slightly increased. In 1869 the Viceroy was made a peer.

Lord Mayo (1869–1872).—During the administration of Lord Mayo, Kabul was convulsed by a war of succession. Neither Sir John Lawrence nor Lord Mayo interfered in the struggle. When the war was concluded and Sher Ali was the indisputable ruler of the country, Lord Mayo invited the Amir to India and entertained him with great pomp at Umballa.

Duke of Edinburgh's Visit.—The Duke of Edinburgh, the second son of the Queen, visited India during this Viceroyalty, and the occasion was marked by a great outburst of loyal feeling throughout the country, the people of which were thus, for the first time, brought into personal contact with the royal family. This visit introduced into the relations of the feudatory princes to the Government an element of personal loyalty to the Crown, which has since become of greatly increased strength and importance. By means of public works Lord Mayo did much to develop the resources of India. He was assassinated at Port Blair, in the Andaman Islands, by a Musalman convict, in 1872.

Lord Northbrook (1872–1876).—Lord Mayo was succeeded as Viceroy by Lord Northbrook, whose policy was marked by wisdom and moderation. A severe famine breaking out in Behar about this time, his lordship appointed Sir Richard Temple to organize measures of relief. In this Sir Richard, who was shortly afterwards made Lieutenant-governor of Bengal, was eminently successful.

Gaekwar of Baroda deposed.—Malhar Rao, the Gaekwar of Baroda, being accused of attempting to poison the Resident at his Court, was tried by a mixed commission of native chiefs and English officers, and deposed for misgovernment and disloyalty. His dominions, however, were bestowed by the Government on a child chosen from the family.

Prince of Wales's Visit.—The Prince of Wales, the eldest son of the Queen and heir to the British throne, visited India in the year 1875, and the preparations that were made for his reception on the occasion were without a parallel for grandeur in the history of India.

Lord Lytton (1876–1880).—Lord Lytton was appointed Viceroy of India in the year 1876. He was the son of a well-known English novelist and politician, and was himself a gifted poet and successful diplomatist. In 1877 the Queen assumed the title of Empress of India. Up to that time, though the paramount ruler in India, she had possessed no distinctive title corresponding to this position, and her assumption of the new style was the formal declaration of her supremacy.

In the same year, a terrible famine broke out in Madras. It extended later to Northern India and caused more wide-spread suffering than any famine for a hundred years. Notwithstanding the most strenuous exertions on the part of the Government it was estimated that several millions died from insufficient food and the diseases resulting therefrom. A quarrel with Kabul led to a war with that country. Lord Lytton became very unpopular with the native section of the Indian press, owing to the passing of the Vernacular Press Act, which interfered with its liberties. He resigned the Viceroyalty in 1880.

Lord Ripon (1880–1884).—Lord Lytton was succeeded by the Marquis of Ripon. He repealed the Vernacular Press Act, and so freed Indian journals from any government restraint on the free discussion of political questions. He introduced a system of self-government, by which the management of local affairs was entrusted to boards locally elected, but his attempt to invest native magistrates with the power of trying Europeans made him very unpopular with the European residents in India. By a further extension of the right of British European subjects to claim to be tried by a jury a satisfactory settlement was arrived at. Lord Ripon re-established the Department of Agriculture and introduced certain needful revenue reforms. He also appointed an Education Commission to devise measures for the further diffusion of popular education.

Lord Dufferin

Lord Dufferin (1884–1888).—Lord Dufferin succeeded Lord Ripon in 1884. Shortly after his arrival in India, he entertained the Amir of Kabul at a grand durbar at Rawalpindi. About this time a Delimitation Commission was appointed, with Sir Peter Lumsden as its president, for the purpose of fixing the boundary between Russia and Afghanistan. But owing to the overbearing conduct of the Russians, an affray occurred between them and the Afghans at Panjdeh, and the relations between the British and Russian Governments became greatly strained in consequence.

Demonstration of Loyalty.—This called forth from the people and the princes of India a surprising manifestation of loyalty to the Government. The feudatory princes placed the entire resources of their states at the disposal of the British Indian Government to be used in case a Russian war should break out. But the tact and ability of Lord Dufferin averted a conflict.

Upper Burma was annexed to the empire in the beginning of 1886. Shortly before this annexation, Lord Dufferin made over the fort of Gwalior to the Maharaja Sindhia; an act of grace which did much to inspire the native princes of India with confidence.

Public Service Commission.—In view of the agitation which prevailed all over India on the question of the appointment of qualified natives to the higher offices in the state, Lord Dufferin appointed a Public Service Commission, and thus set the question at rest. When the Queen-Empress completed the fiftieth year of her reign, in the year 1887, a Jubilee was held with great pomp to celebrate the event. Throughout India there was universal enthusiasm. Lord Dufferin on his retirement (1888) was created Marquis of Dufferin and Ava.

Lord Lansdowne (1888–1893).—One of the principal events of Lord Lansdowne's administration was the Manipur war in 1891. Tikendrajit, the Senapati of Manipur, having murdered five Englishmen, including the Chief Commissioner of Assam, a British force was sent to Manipur. The Raja was deposed and the Senapati executed, but the Government declined to annex the state. A young member of a distant branch of the Raja's family was placed on the throne, and the British Commissioner appointed to rule the country for him during his minority. Great attention was given during this viceroyalty to the strengthening of the defences of the north-western frontier. Lord Lansdowne, having completed his term of office, returned to England in 1893.

Lord Elgin (1894–1899).—Lord Lansdowne was succeeded in the Viceroyalty by Lord Elgin, the son of that Lord Elgin who died at Dharmsala in 1862.

During his administration there occurred a series of grave calamities. Plague broke out in 1896; and though its ravages have been checked, the country is not yet free from it. This was followed in 1897 by a famine, which affected nearly a third of the total population of India. Thanks to the wisdom and energy of the authorities, and to the generous aid of the people of other parts of the British Empire, the worst consequences of the famine were averted. The damages caused by the earthquake, which swept from Calcutta over North-Eastern Bengal and Assam, carrying death and ruin to hundreds of towns and villages, were quickly repaired.

War on North-West Frontier.—During the Elgin administration the peace of the North-West Frontier was much disturbed. In consequence of a disturbance at Chitral a military expedition was sent into that country, and ultimately a British garrison was placed there, and a road was made from Peshawar through the intervening tribal territories. These operations were followed by a succession of tribal risings, the most formidable of them being that of the Afridis, which led to a military expedition on a large scale being sent into that country.

Diamond Jubilee.—In commemoration of the completion of the sixtieth year of the reign of the Queen-Empress, a Diamond Jubilee was celebrated throughout India in 1897. The celebrations everywhere were of the most enthusiastic and loyal character, notably at Gwalior, where the Maharaja remitted 60 lakhs of revenue and set free ten per cent of the prisoners.

Lord Curzon (1899–1905).—Lord Curzon succeeded Lord Elgin in 1899. He was the Viceroy and Governor-general of India for seven years. A nobleman of great learning who travelled much, he had visited India several times before he became its supreme ruler. He saw that the frontier tribes beyond the Indus often gave great trouble to the Government, and that it was difficult to rule the districts beyond the Indus from Lahore, so he constituted these districts into a Chief-commissionership under the name of the North-Western Frontier Province, and changed the name of the North-Western

Provinces into that of the United Province of Agra and Oudh.

Proclamation of Edward VII.—During his administration, on the 23rd January, 1901, the Queen-Empress died. All India mourned the loss of the great Queen, whom everyone regarded as his mother. There were great demonstrations of sorrow. People went about barefooted, fed the poor, wore black, and showed their sorrow in a variety of other ways.

King-Emperor Edward VII

Queen Alexandra

After a year of mourning came the coronation of the King-Emperor, Edward the VII. His illness on the eve of the coronation postponed the event for a short time. A great Durbar was held at Delhi, where all the feudatory chiefs attended, and an elephant procession took place which exceeded in magnificence anything of the kind witnessed before.

Famine Commission.—In the early part of his Viceroyalty, Lord Curzon very successfully coped with a severe famine. To find out what could be done to prevent such calamities he appointed a Famine Commission, in which our illustrious countryman Ray Kauhchandra Nurkherji Bahadur had a seat.

Mission to Tibet.—In the early years of the East India Company in Bengal, the British maintained friendly relations with Tibet and the neighbouring mountain countries. In 1768 the Gurkhas conquered Nepal and introduced the policy of exclusion of all foreigners. The British, engaged in wars and reforms in India, could not pay much attention to their relations with the Himalayan states. Some attempts were made from time to time to open up friendly commercial relations with Tibet, but the Tibetans stoutly resisted all advances. On the part of the Indian Government, Lord Curzon despatched a peaceful commercial mission. This the Tibetans resisted. But they were at last obliged to admit the mission, which reached Lhasa, the capital. The Dalai Lama fled to Mongolia, and the officers in command of the mission made a convention with the Tisu Lama and placed him in charge of the Tibetan Government.

Educational Reform.—Two of Lord Curzon's measures elicited much hostile criticism in India. The first was his scheme of Educational Reform, and the second his scheme for the Partition of Bengal.

Lord Curzon called a meeting at Simla of the heads of the various Education Departments in India, and discussed with them the question of Education and the educational needs of the various provinces. These settled, he appointed the Universities Commission to settle the question of High Education. Then a bill was introduced in the Imperial Legislative Council for the advancement of education in India, and it was passed in the shape of the Universities Act.

Lieutenant-Governorship of Eastern Bengal and Assam.—The Lieutenant-Governor of Bengal complained of the hard work he had to do in administering so great and populous a province as Bengal, and so Lord Curzon transferred three entire divisions of Bengal to the Province of Assam and created it a new Lieutenant-Governorship.

Difference with Secretary of State.—There was formerly in the Viceregal Executive Council a member who advised the Viceroy on all military matters. His opinions often clashed with those of the Commander-in-Chief. At the instance of Lord Kitchener, the military membership was abolished, and the Commander-in-Chief made the sole adviser of Government in all military matters except in the matter of military supplies, for which a new member was appointed.

Lord Curzon was opposed to the change, but in this matter the Secretary of State did not support him and so he resigned, and Lord Minto, a descendant of the Lord Minto who ruled India from 1807–12, was appointed in his place.

Lord Minto, 1905.—Lord Minto takes his steps with great caution. He is trying his best to cool down the feeling roused by the changes introduced by Lord Curzon.

Berar belonged to the Nizam, but he was obliged to cede it to the Government of India to meet the pay of the Hyderabad contingent, subject to the conditions that the surplus revenue should be paid to him. It used to be governed by the Resident of Hyderabad as commissioner. Lord Curzon made a final settlement with the Nizam and transferred the country to the Central Provinces, the Nizam receiving in lieu of the surplus revenues a certain fixed annual amount.

CHAPTER III

BRITISH ADMINISTRATION

The Governor-General's Powers.—The British Indian Administration is presided over by a Viceroy of the King of Great Britain and Ireland, the Governor-General of India. He is all-powerful in India. He is the head of the Military and the Civil Administration; but is responsible to the Secretary of State for India. The latter, who is assisted by a Council of veteran Anglo-Indian officers of long standing, looks after the Indian Administration in Britain. The Secretary of State for India is a member of the Privy-Council and of the Cabinet or Government of Great Britain. He is supported by the Prime Minister and the other members of the Cabinet, and is responsible for every act in connection with the government of India to the British Parliament. He is a member of Parliament either in the Lords or in the Commons. The latter consists of over six hundred representatives of the people, who meet together to deliberate on public affairs, and to make laws.

Their Limitations.—Thus the Governor-General of India, though possessed of unlimited powers, cannot do as he pleases. He is responsible to the Secretary of State and through him to the Parliament. Such is the sense of justice of the British nation, that for certain supposed wrongs done in the course of his administration of affairs the greatest of Governors-General, Warren Hastings, was impeached and had to undergo his trial. The trial lasted for seven years, and though Hastings was acquitted, the cost of the proceedings nearly ruined him. Another of the Viceroys was recalled, not by the Parliament but by the Board of Control, which before the year 1858 exercised the same power as the Secretary of State does at present. Even Clive, the founder of the British Empire in India, had to suffer a parliamentary enquiry into his conduct of affairs.

The Executive Council.—The Governor-General is assisted in his administration by an Executive Council of five members, the Supply Member, a Law Member, a Finance Member, a Home Member, and a Public Works Member. The Commander-in-Chief is always an extraordinary member of the Council. The Governor-General himself manages all the foreign affairs of the Indian Empire with the assistance of the Foreign Secretary. The other members also are assisted by secretaries in their own departments. The Governor-General, however, is not bound to accept the views of any particular member, or even the views of all the members combined. He can do on his own responsibility whatever he thinks fit, the members have only the right to record their dissent. But behind there is, as we have seen, the control of the Secretary of State for India and of the British Parliament. There are eighteen departments, of which four or five are principal departments. The Commander-in-Chief is at the head of the army. He is supreme in the army and in the field, but the voice of the Viceroy is supreme in peace and war.

Madras and Bombay.—The Governor-General has two subordinate governments, viz. those of Madras and Bombay. These are presided over by Governors sent from England, who, like the Viceroy himself, are assisted by an Executive Council. For making laws, that is, for the formation of a legislative council, the Governor-General adds to his Executive Council certain representatives of the people of the various provinces. He adds also the Governor of the province in which the council happens to be held. The Governors of Bombay and Madras are in a like way assisted in making laws by popular representatives.

Lieutenant-Governors and Commissioners.—It has already been said that by the Regulating Act of 1773, the Governor of Bengal was made the Governor-General of India. At the time of that act the Governor of Bengal was the Dewan of Bengal and Behar, but gradually, as the British Indian Empire extended and the responsibilities of the Governor-General increased, the work became too much for a single individual. In 1836 it was proposed to make Agra the seat of a government, with a Governor of the Bombay type. But subsequently the idea was given up, and a Lieutenant-Governor was appointed to rule the North-Western Provinces. Bengal long continued to be ruled by the senior member of the Council of the Governor-General, who was termed Deputy-Governor. From 1856, however, Bengal also was constituted into a Lieutenant-Governorship. Later, the Punjab and Burma were placed under Lieutenant-Governors, and recently East Bengal and Assam have been given a Lieutenant-Governor. The Chief Commissioner of the Central Provinces is under the direct control of the Viceroy, so are the Commissioners of Ajmir, Coorg, British Baluchistan, and the Andamans.

Residents and Agents.—For the supervision of the affairs of the Native State there are different arrangements. The great and important states have each a Resident of its own, who advises the Governor-General on all matters relating to that state. In addition, as representative of the paramount power, he is recognized as the chief adviser of the native sovereign. To this class of states belong Hyderabad, Mysore, Kashmir, &c. The Resident of Mysore is practically the ruler of Mysore during the minority of the Raja. There is an Agent of the Governor-General at Abu, who keeps an eye on the administration of the Rajputana states. The principal Rajput states have in addition Residents under the Agent placed in their capitals, and the minor states are supervised by the Agent himself and his officers. There is another Agent of the Governor-General at Mhow, who overlooks the administration of the states in Central India, the big ones through Residents placed in their capital and the smaller ones through his own officers.

Small states are placed under local administrations, the District Officer or the Commissioner acts as political officer.

Lieutenant-Governors, Commissioners, and District Officers.—The Lieutenant-Governors have no Executive Councils. They are assisted by Secretaries, who, with a certain number of official and non-official members, some elected, some nominated, constitute the Legislative Council. The Acts passed in these councils must be confirmed by the Governor-General in Council before they become law. The Lieutenant-Governors are selected by the Governor-General from amongst the members of the Indian Civil Service. For purposes of administration, each Local Government has a number of Commissioners under it, and the Commissioners, in their turn, have a number of District Officers under them. The districts are the real administrative units, and the District Officers are really the most important functionaries under the British administration. They are responsible for the peace of their districts. They collect the revenues of the district; they superintend the jails, the hospitals, the municipalities, and the primary schools; they initiate sanitary reforms and suggest and erect works of public utility, and they preside over the various committees concerned with the district administration.

The Supreme Courts.—By the acceptance of the Dewani the East India Company became the receivers of the taxes and the head of the civil administration, and the Governor-General in Council became the highest court of appeal in all civil and fiscal matters. Then the Governor-General's work multiplied, and he delegated the civil appeals to a court of appellate justice known as the Sadr Diwany Adalat, or chief civil court, and he made the Board of Revenue supreme in all fiscal matters. When the Nizamat was transferred to the Company, the Governor-General in Council became the highest court of appeal in criminal matters also; and he delegated his functions to a Sadr Nizamat Adalat, or chief criminal court.

How they were Founded.—The Supreme Court was founded by the Regulating Act for administering British Law in the Capitals of India. So during the whole period of the Company's government there were three courts of justice. When the British sovereign assumed the direct control of Indian affairs these three courts were formed into a High Court, which received its charter from the sovereign. There are four chartered High Courts in India, viz. those of Calcutta, Madras, Bombay, and Allahabad. The Chief Court of Lahore and the Court of the Recorder at Rangoon have been established by the Governor-General in Council.

The Inferior Courts.—The High Courts are assisted in the administration of justice by District Judges, who dispose of the less important matters of appeal, and of all appeals as to matters of fact. They also take original cognizance of various sorts of civil cases, and supervise the administration of justice by their Native subordinates, subordinate Judges and Munsifs. These District Judges are often Session Judges, and with the assistance of Jurors or Assessors try all criminal cases of a grave nature. They can pass sentences of capital punishment, but in this matter their sentence is subject to confirmation by the High Court.

The Laws and the Highest Court.—In theory Hindus and Muhammadans are subject in civil and criminal matters to their own civil and criminal codes; but gradually the British Indian Legislature has passed Acts incorporating the substance of these codes, and by these the people are governed. In matters of inheritance, adoption, &c., however, Hindus and Musalmans are governed by their own old laws. The High Court, it must be remembered, is not the highest court of judicature for British India. Appeals may be made from its decisions to the Judicial Committee of the Privy-Council, which must therefore be considered the highest tribunal for India, as for the rest of the empire.

Early Ideas on Education.—The idea which guided the British Administration of India in earlier days was one of absolute non-intervention in matters educational. They thought if Government offered to educate the people, it would be looked upon with suspicion, and the people would be disaffected; so beyond giving monthly grants to Pundits and Maulvis here and there, no attempt was made for several decades to encourage education.

In 1781 the Madrassa College was established at Calcutta, and in 1791 a Sanskrit College at Benares, education being imparted through the medium of the Oriental classics. In 1824 the Calcutta Sanskrit College was established on the model of the Sanskrit College previously established at Benares. But by this time there was a great need in the country of an English education. The rulers' speech was English. The judges spoke English and the merchants used English. They had to be approached, talked to, and otherwise communicated with. English schools were started by private individuals. These were established for the training of clerks, writers, and other native officers of the State. In the thirties the Government resolved to impart education to the people, and there arose a conflict of opinions as to the aims and means of giving such an education. Some advocated the propriety of the Government supplying a purely English education, some held that Persian and Arabic should be taught in the schools, and others that the education given should be entirely in the vernacular. The party contending for an English education prevailed, and the Government established many English schools in different parts of the country.

Organization of Education.—In the forties, Government resolved to impart education to the masses through the medium of the native tongues, and, with that end in view, a number of Model Schools and Circle Schools were established. The great charter of popular education for India was, however, Sir Charles Wood's Despatch of 1854. The Despatch established Universities at Calcutta, Madras, and Bombay. It organized educational departments in the various provinces of the empire, and appointed Inspectors of Schools to preside over circles of four or five districts. Colleges, too, were established for imparting higher education. Degrees were instituted by the Universities, and conferred upon students after testing their acquirements.

Scientific Education.—Higher education was confined at first to Literature and Philosophy, with some Mathematics. In the seventies, Science began to be cultivated, and at this moment there exist means for imparting scientific knowledge of which the Government may very well be proud.

CHAPTER IV

THE EFFECTS OF BRITISH RULE IN INDIA

Duration of Peace in Different Parts.—British rule has given India what she never enjoyed before, namely, abiding tranquillity. Peace extends throughout the length and breadth of the country, and has lasted in many places for more than a century. The din of battle has not been heard in Bengal and Behar since the days of Mir Kasim, or in Guzerat since the second Marhatta war. Southern India has enjoyed profound peace since the death of Tipu Sultan in 1799, and the Deccan and Central India since the removal of Baji Rao and Appa Saheb from their capitals, Poona and Nagpur. The Punjab and Sindh, Assam and Burma, have experienced very little disturbance since their conquest. Once only during the century was the peace of Hindustan disturbed, and that was by the Sepoy Mutiny, which, as we have seen, was promptly and effectually quelled in little more than twelve months.

Removal of Causes of War.—Two fruitful sources of trouble, which greatly disturbed the Mughal empire, have altogether ceased to exist under British rule, the ambition of provincial governors to extend their authority, and the constant struggles between rival candidates at every succession to the imperial dignity. Wars of succession have been unknown in Britain for centuries, and the system under which viceroys and governors of provinces are changed every fifth year, and subordinate officers more frequently, checks ambition in high places, and tends to prevent anyone from acquiring too dangerous a local influence.

Civilization of Wild Tribes.—The wild tribes of India, who were a constant source of disturbance of the peace, are being rapidly reclaimed. The Garos, Kukis, Khasias, Nagas, Bhils, Kols, Ramusis, Santals, Mairs, Minas, Gonds, and Orangs, have all felt the influence of civilized rule, and are fast settling down as peaceful agriculturists and honest labourers. The mountain fastnesses of the Himalayas, the Vindhyas, the Sahyadri (W. Ghats), and the Nilgiris, which perpetually sent forth into the plains disturbers of the peace, have now been completely brought under control, and these once barely accessible regions have become the sites for a number of health and pleasure resorts, such as Simla, Darjeeling, Nainital, Mari, Shillong, Mussoorie, Mahabaleshwar, and Utakamand.

Improved Means of Communication.—Another blessing which British rule has conferred upon India is facility of communication between different parts of the country. Nations that were not even known to one another by name, have now become friends and neighbours. By the railway the remotest corner of India may be reached from the capital in the course of four or five days; and through the telegraph a message can be sent to any distance in half an hour. Formerly, while one part of India reaped a superabundant crop, and the people had no means of disposing of the surplus, another part was, perhaps, the scene of a devastating famine. But improved communications have facilitated the distribution of food-stuffs, and famine is becoming more and more rare.

Blessings of a Strong Government.—India has always required a strong government; and no government India ever had was as strong as that of the British. It has not only secured India from foreign invasion, but it has checked all violent and organized crime. The Thugs, who, in the name of religion, committed the grossest atrocities on travellers, have been almost extirpated, and dacoits have been put down with a strong hand. The dacoits of Bengal, the Pindaris of Central India, and the various marauding tribes that lived by plunder and violence, have been compelled to take to peaceful occupations, a blessing to themselves, though an even greater blessing to others.

Sanitary Improvements.—Pestilence was another scourge of India, which swept away millions at a time from different localities. Ancient India stood aghast at these terrible visitations, and sought remedies for them in prayer and worship. The Brahmans, indeed, laid down minute rules of conduct, called *Acharas*, by the strict observance of which individuals might avert these calamities and attain to longevity. But it was reserved for the British Government to grapple successfully with these periodical visitations by draining marshes, supplying the urban population with filtered water, and establishing organized systems of conservancy. No Government has ever bestowed more attention on the task of securing the lives and properties of its subjects, not only from foreign and domestic enemies, but also from the ravages of disease. An enlightened Government does not rest content merely with protecting the lives and properties of its subjects, but it endeavours also to so arrange matters that the people may, if they choose, be both happy and contented.

Economic Changes.—British rule has, indeed, wrought a great revolution in the economy of the country. Industries, which were the pride and glory of India, and all her fine arts, have dwindled into insignificance owing to European competition, backed as it has been by modern machinery. The manufacture of cloth, whether woollen, silk, or cotton, and of cutlery, has fallen mainly into the hands of Europeans. This is a serious change, and one that was fraught with immense suffering to those whose occupations were thus taken away. But the lack of employment caused by the introduction of foreign manufactures has been more than compensated by the flow of British capital into the country. This has enabled India to undertake gigantic railway works, and to establish the cotton, jute, tea, and indigo industries, affording occupation to millions of the natives of India. The industrial revolution of the eighteenth and nineteenth centuries caused by the application of machinery to manufactures has everywhere substituted the productions of the factory for that of the cottage or the workshop.

Educational Improvement.—The greatest glory of British rule in India, however, is the noble attempt that is being made to educate the masses. Education was, in all the preceding periods, confined to the higher classes. The masses were steeped in ignorance and superstition, but British rule has established vernacular schools in almost every village, affording opportunities to all classes of the people to improve their minds. Popular education is given through the medium of the vernacular, and higher education through the medium of English. No distinction is made of caste, colour, or creed in the steps thus taken for the diffusion of knowledge. A great impetus has also been given to the study of the classical literature of India. Sanskrit classical works, which had long lain buried in oblivion, are being searched for, published, studied, commented upon, and translated,—revealing the part which, during four thousand years, civilization has played in the various departments of Indian life. At the same time, a prose literature has sprung up in almost all the vernaculars, which has a large field for improvement and usefulness before it.

Religious Neutrality.—The policy of strict neutrality in religious matters is another excellent feature of British rule in India. This has given rise to many new religions. Raja Ram Mohon Ray founded the Brahmo Samaj, the members of which are strict monotheists. His great successor was the late Kesav Chandra Sen, who carried the ideas of the founder a little further. Dayananda Sarasvati, who founded the Aryya Samaj, also believed in one God. The Musalmans also have developed a new reform under the name of *Farazi.* Christian missionaries of various denominations have done much good in diffusing education. The names of Schwartz, Carey, Marshman, Ward, and Duff deserve all honour from the people of India.

Self-government.—The history of India in the past is the history of great individuals. Indian people seem almost incapable of united action. Under the fostering care of their present rulers, who are noted for their capacity for such action, they are, however, being made to understand its value. The Government of India has recently given the people the privilege of electing representatives on Municipal and District Boards, and even in the Universities; and the Legislative Councils have lately been remodelled so as to include a fair number of the representatives of the people.

Its Expansion.—The policy of Lord William Bentinck, who was the first to admit the natives of India to responsible offices of the state, has undergone gradual expansion, culminating in the Public Service Commission, which has thrown open to them all the higher positions in the Service with the exception of a few of the most important appointments, reserved exclusively for the members of the British race. Natives can now aspire to high offices in the Administrative Service without going to England.

Legal Rights.—Under British rule every man is equal in the eye of the law, and the Indian Judiciary has a high reputation for its incorruptibility and for its judicial capacity. India appreciates the value of these and sincerely desires the long continuance of British rule.

A CHRONOLOGICAL TABLE OF THE PRINCIPAL EVENTS IN INDIAN HISTORY

B.C.

557. The birth of Buddha.
521. Persian invasion under Darius.
477. Death of Buddha.
467. Death of Mahavira, the founder of the Jaina religion.
327. Invasion of India by Alexander.
320. Chandra Gupta rises to power.
312. Chandra Gupta is made king.
312 to 307. Megasthenes at Pataliputra.
292. The death of Chandra Gupta.
264. Bindusar dies, and Asoka comes to power.
260. Asoka ascends the throne.
256. The Bactrian kingdom founded.
223. Asoka dies.
71. The Andhras conquer Magadha.
56. Beginning of the Malwa era or Samwat.

A.D.

50. Gondopherus, king in the Punjab.
78. Kanishka becomes emperor. Beginning of the Saka era.
319. Beginning of the Nepal or Gupta era.
468. The last mention of Skanda Gupta.
510. The last mention of Bhanu Gupta.
533. Yasodharmadev expels the Hunas. The battle of Korur.
607. Harshavardhan ascends the throne of Kanauj.
627 to 642. Hiouen Thsang in India.
672. Aditya Sen of Magadha declares himself independent.
711 to 760. The first Muhammadan conquest under Kasim.
744. The fall of the Valabhis.
746. The foundation of the city of Anahilpattan and of the dynasty of Chapotkatas.
752. The Rashtrakutas overthrow the Chalukyas of Vatapi.
943. The Chalukyas come to power in Guzerat.
977. Subuktigin ascends the throne of Ghazni.
997. Subuktigin dies, and Mahmud ascends the throne.
1001. First invasion of Mahmud.
1006. Raja Bhoj becomes king of Malwa.
1008. Fourth invasion of Mahmud.

A.D.

1017. Fifth invasion of Mahmud.

1023. Tenth invasion of Mahmud and the annexation of the Punjab to the Ghazni empire.

1024. Twelfth invasion of Mahmud.

1026. Mahmud destroys the temple of Somnath.

1030. Death of Mahmud.

1036. Re-building of the temple of Somnath by Bhimadev of Guzerat.

1062. Death of Raja Bhoj.

1066. Conversion of Tibet by Dipankar Srijnana.

1081. Chola conquest of Orissa. Building of the temple of Jagannath.

1119. Beginning of the Lakshmana Sen Era.

1176. Muhammad of Ghor conquers the town of Uch in the Punjab.

1186. Muhammad of Ghor takes possession of Lahore.

1189. Yadava Bhillama conquers Kalyana.

1191. Muhammad of Ghor defeated by Prithi Roy.

1193. Prithi Roy defeated and killed.

1194. Muhammad of Ghor invades Kanauj, defeats Jay Chandra, and annexes Kanauj and Benares.

1197. Bakhtiyar Khiliji conquers Behar.

1199. Bengal conquered by Bakhtiyar.

1202. The Baghelas expel Muhammadans from Guzerat and overthrow the Chalukya dynasty.

1205. Muhammad of Ghor killed by the Gakkhars of the Punjab.

1232. Sultan Altamsh sacks Ujjayini and destroys the famous temple of Mahakala.

1288. The fall of the Slave Kings. The Khilijis come to power.

1295. Alauddin Khiliji ascends the throne of Delhi.

1297. „ „ annexes Guzerat and Malwa.

1310. „ „ conquers the Deccan.

1316. Death of Alauddin Khiliji.

1321. The end of the Khilijis. The Tughlaks come to power.

1325. Muhammad Tughlak ascends the throne.

1336. Foundation of the Hindu kingdom of Vijayanagar (Bukka Family).

1337. Rebellion of the Amirani Sada.

1345. Haji Ilias declares the independence of Bengal.

1347. The Deccan declares itself independent. The foundation of the Bahmani kingdom.

1351. Death of Muhammad Tughlak and the succession of Firoz Tughlak.

1394. Malik-us-Shark declares himself independent at Jaunpur.

1396. Guzerat asserts its independence.

1398. Invasion of Timur.

1401. Malwa asserts its independence.

1412. The extinction of the Pathan empire.

1424. Annexation of the Kakateya kingdom by the Bahmanis.

A.D.

1478. Bahlol Lodi annexes Jaunpur.

1481. Assassination of Mahmud Gawan.

1487. Narasinha becomes king of Vijayanagar.

1489. Bijapur and Berar established as independent kingdoms.

1491. Foundation of the kingdom of Ahmadnagar.

1494. Annexation of Behar by Sikandar Lodi.

" Alauddin Husain Shah ascends the throne of Bengal.

1498. Vasco da Gama lands at Calicut.

1500. Foundation of Agra by Sikandar Lodi.

1512. Foundation of the Golconda kingdom.

1516. Death of Sikandar Lodi.

1526. Invasion of Babar. End of the Lodis. End of the Bahmanis. Bidar becomes an independent kingdom.

" First battle of Panipat.

1527. Battle of Sikri.

1529. Conquest of Chitor by Bahadur Shah of Guzerat.

1530. Death of Babar and succession of Humayun.

1536. Malwa annexed to Guzerat.

1540. Humayun defeated by Sher Shah, who ascends the throne of Delhi.

1542. Birth of Akbar.

1555. Humayun re-conquers Delhi.

1556. Second battle of Panipat.

1557. Death of Bahadur Shah of Guzerat.

1560. Akbar begins to reign independently.

1563. Sulaiman Kirani establishes his independence in Bengal.

1565. Battle of Talikot.

" Annexation of Orissa by Kalapahar.

1568. Conquest of Chitor by Akbar.

1572. Berar ceases to be an independent kingdom.

" Guzerat made over to Akbar.

1575. Bengal annexed to the Mughal empire by Akbar.

1599. Establishment of the East India Company.

1605. Death of Akbar and succession of Jahangir.

1615. Arrival of Sir Thomas Roe in India.

1627. Death of Jahangir and succession of Shah Jahan.

" Birth of Sivaji.

1636. Ahmadnagar annexed to the Mughal empire.

1639. Foundation of Madras.

1658. Battle of Ujjayini and the defeat of Yasovanta Singh.

1659. Battle of Kajoa.

" Dara betrayed into the hands of Aurangzeb and sentenced to death.

" Aurangzeb ascends the throne.

1664. Sivaji assumes the title of Raja.

1666. Aurangzeb's treaty with Sivaji and Sivaji's visit to Delhi.

A.D.

1668. Bombay made over to the East India Company.
1670. Sivaji's war with the Mughals.
1671. Re-imposition of the Jazia.
1674. Sivaji assumes the title of Maharaja.
1680. Death of Sivaji and the accession of Sambhaji.
1683. Aurangzeb marches to conquer the Deccan.
1689. Sambhaji sentenced to death and accession of Sivaji II.
1698. Fort William is built.
" The fall of Ginji.
1700. The death of Raja Ram.
1704. Foundation of Murshidabad.
1707. Death of Aurangzeb and accession of Bahadur Shah.
1708. Release of Sahu. Marhatta Civil War.
" Assassination of Guru Govinda.
1712. Death of Bahadur Shah and accession of Farukhsiyar.
" Balaji Bisvanath Bhatta founds the Peshwa family.
1717. Treaty of the Mughals with Raja Sahu.
1719. Death of Farukhsiyar and accession of Muhammad Shah.
1720. Baji Rao becomes Peshwa.
1721. The Nizam revolts.
1728. The Nizam makes peace with Baji Rao.
1730. Kolhapur made a separate kingdom. End of the Marhatta Civil War.
1731. Battle of Dubhoy.
1738. Baji Rao obtains Malwa.
1739. Invasion of Nadir Shah.
1740. Death of Baji Rao and the succession of Balaji Baji Rao.
" Ali Vardi Khan becomes viceroy of Bengal.
1742. Invasion of Bengal by Raghaji Bhonsla.
1748. First invasion of Ahmad Shah Abdali.
" Death of Muhammad Shah and accession of Ahmad Shah.
" Death of Raja Sahu and removal of the Peshwa to Poona.
" Death of the first Nizam.
1751. Second invasion of Ahmad Shah Abdali.
1752. Clive's defence of Arkot.
" Cession of Orissa to the Marhattas.
1754. Death of Ahmad Shah and accession of Alamgir II.
1755. Conquest of Guzerat by the Marhattas.
1756. Third invasion of Ahmad Shah Abdali.
" Death of Ali Vardi Khan and succession of Sirajuddaula.
" The Massacre of Black Hole of Calcutta.
1757. The battle of Plassey.
1758. The Marhattas conquer Lahore.
1759. Loss of French influence in the Deccan.

A.D.

1759. Fourth invasion of Ahmad Shah Abdali.
" Shah Alam II proclaims himself emperor.
" Sadasiva Rao obtains Ahmadnagar.
" Hyder Ali invades the Karnatik (First Maisur War).
1760. Clive returns to England.
" Hyder Ali becomes Sultan of Maisur.
1761. Capture of Pondicherry by the English.
" Third battle of Panipat.
" Death of Balaji Baji Rao and succession of Madhava Rao.
1762. Sikh conquest of the Punjab.
1763. Madhava Rao proceeds against Hyder Ali.
" Battles of Udvanala and Gheria.
1764. Battle of Baxar.
1765. Grant of the Divani of Bengal, Behar, and Orissa to the East India Company.
" Shah Alam II agrees to live under British protection.
1771. Bisvaji Krishna invades Hindustan. Shah Alam II renounces British protection and proceeds to Delhi.
" Death of Madhava Rao and succession of Madhava Rao Narayan.
1772. Warren Hastings as Governor. Narayan Rao murdered.
1774. The Rohilla war.
1775. First Marhatta war.
1776. Treaty of Purandar.
1779. Second Marhatta war.
" Convention of Wadgaon.
1780. Hastings quarrels with Chait Singh.
" Second Maisur war.
1782. Treaty of Salbai.
" Death of Hyder.
1783. Treaty of Mangalore.
1784. Pitt's India Bill passed.
1785. Hastings returns to England, and Sir John Macpherson becomes governor-general.
1786. Lord Cornwallis appointed governor-general.
1787. Shah Alam II blinded by Ghulam Kadir. Sindhia supreme in Hindustan.
1790. Triple Alliance against Tipu Sultan.
1790–92. Third Maisur war.
1792. Chinese invasion of Nepal.
1793. The Permanent Settlement and the return of Lord Cornwallis to England. Sir John Shore governor-general.
1795. Battle of Kurdla.
" Suicide of Madhava Rao Narayan and succession of Baji Rao II.
1798. Marquis of Wellesley, governor-general.

A.D.

1799. The policy of Subsidiary Alliance started.

" Fourth Maisur War and restoration of the Hindu dynasty in Maisur.

1800. Death of Nana Farnavis.

1801. Ranjit Singh assumes the title of Maharaja.

1802. Treaty of Bassein.

1803. Third Marhatta war. Battle of Assai.

" Battle of Laswari.

" Battle of Argaon.

1804. The English become the paramount power in India.

" War with Holkar.

1805. Lord Cornwallis comes to India a second time.

" Death of Lord Cornwallis at Ghazipur. Lord Minto appointed governor-general.

1806. The Vellore mutiny. Death of Shah Alam.

1809. The Sikh chiefs to the east of the Sutlej place themselves under British protection.

1813. Lord Minto leaves India. The Marquis of Hastings appointed governor-general.

1813–15. The Nepal war.

1817. Pindari war. Battle of Mehidpur.

1818. Fourth Marhatta war. Baji Rao overthrown.

1823. The Marquis of Hastings returns to England. Lord Amherst sent out as governor-general.

1824. The first Burmese war.

1826. Cession of Assam, Arakan, and Tenasserim to the English.

" Capture of Bharatpur.

1828–1835. Lord William Bentinck, governor-general.

1836. Lord Auckland, governor-general.

" The first Afghan war.

1838. Afghan War.

1839. Death of Ranajit Singh.

1841. Sir Alexander Burnes killed.

1842. Massacre of British troops.

" Lord Ellenborough appointed governor-general.

" Dost Muhammad returns to Kabul.

1843. The Sind war.

" The Gwalior war.

1844. Retirement of Lord Ellenborough, Lord Hardinge, governor-general.

1845. Battles of Mudki and Ferozpur.

1846. Battle of Aliwal.

" Battle of Sobraon.

" Treaty of Mian Mir.

1848. Retirement of Lord Hardinge. Lord Dalhousie, governor-general.

A.D.

1848. The second Sikh war.

1849. Capture of Multan.

" Battle of Chillianwala.

" Battle of Guzerat.

" Annexation of the Punjab.

1852. The second Burmese war.

1853. Annexation of Jhansi and Nagpur.

1856. Annexation of Oudh.

" Retirement of Lord Dalhousie and the appointment of Lord Canning.

" Wars with China and Persia.

1857. The Sepoy Mutiny.

1858. Assumption of direct administration by the queen.

" The queen's proclamation issued.

1862. Lord Canning leaves India.

1862–63. Lord Elgin.

1864. Lord Lawrence appointed governor-general.

" The Bhutan war.

1869. Lord Mayo appointed governor-general.

1872. Assassination of Lord Mayo.

" Lord Northbrook, governor-general.

1875. The visit of the Prince of Wales.

1876. Lord Lytton appointed governor-general.

1877. The queen assumes the title of Empress of India.

1878. The second Afghan war.

1879. The Treaty of Gandamak.

1879–80. The third Afghan war.

1880–84. Lord Ripon.

1884–88. Lord Dufferin.

1886. Annexation of Burma.

1887. Queen Victoria's Jubilee.

1888–93. Lord Lansdowne.

1891. The Manipur war.

1893. Lord Elgin appointed governor-general.

1895. Chitral expedition.

1897–98. Tirah expedition.

1897. Queen Victoria's Diamond Jubilee.

1899. Lord Curzon governor-general.

1901. New North-west Frontier Province.

1902. Indian Princes received by King and Queen.

1903. Coronation Durbar held on 1st January.

1904. Mission to Tibet.

1905. Severe earthquake in Northern India. Provinces of Bengal and Assam reconstituted.

" Lord Minto governor-general.

BRITISH GOVERNORS-GENERAL OF INDIA UNDER THE EAST INDIA COMPANY

A.D.

1774. Warren Hastings.
1785. Sir John Macpherson (officiating).
1786. Earl (afterwards Marquis of) Cornwallis.
1793. Sir John Shore.
1798. Earl of Mornington (Marquis of Wellesley).
1805. Marquis of Cornwallis (second time).
" Sir George Barlow (temporary).
1807. Lord (afterwards Earl of) Minto.
1813. Earl of Moira (Marquis of Hastings).
1823. John Adam (officiating).
" Lord (afterwards Earl of) Amherst.
1828. Lord William Cavendish Bentinck.
1835. Sir Charles Metcalfe (afterwards Lord Metcalfe, temporary).
1836. Lord (afterwards Earl of) Auckland.
1842. Lord (afterwards Earl of) Ellenborough.
1844. Sir Henry (afterwards Viscount) Hardinge.
1848. Earl (afterwards Marquis) of Dalhousie.
1856. Viscount (afterwards Earl) Canning.

VICEROYS UNDER THE CROWN

1858. Earl Canning.
1862. Lord Elgin.
1863. Sir William Denison (officiating).
1864. Sir John Lawrence (afterwards Lord Lawrence).
1869. Earl of Mayo.
1872. Lord (afterwards Earl of) Northbrook.
1876. Lord (afterwards Earl of) Lytton.
1880. Marquis of Ripon.
1884. Earl of Dufferin (afterwards Marquis of Dufferin and Ava).
1888. Marquis of Lansdowne.
1893. Lord Elgin.
1899. Lord Curzon.
1905. Lord Minto.